THE 6-STAGE PROBATE PROCESS

How to Navigate California Probate

FIRST EDITION
R. SAM PRICE
CALIFORNIA PROBATE ATTORNEY

Copyright © 2024 by ProbateDocs LLC. All rights reserved.

Published by ProbateDocs LLC.

www.probatedocs.com

Printed in the United States of America.

Except as permitted under the United States Copyright Act of 1976, no part of this publication may be reproduced or distributed in any form or by any means, electronic, mechanical, photocopying, recording, scanning, or otherwise, or stored in a database or retrieval system, without the prior written permission of the publisher.

Requests to the publisher for permission should be addressed to:

ProbateDocs LLC

454 Cajon Street

Redlands, CA 92373

hello@probatedocs.com

This publication is designed to provide accurate and authoritative information in regard to the subject matter covered. It is sold with the understanding that the publisher is not engaged in rendering legal, accounting, or other professional services. If legal or other expert assistance is required, the services of a competent professional person should be sought.

—from the declaration of principles jointly adopted by a committee of the American Bar Association and a committee of publishers

TABLE OF CONTENTS

ABOUT THE AUTHOR XV

THE 6-STAGE PROBATE PROCESS™ 1
Stage 1 Starting the Probate Case™ 1
Stage 2 Appointing the Personal Representative™ 1
Stage 3 Estate Administration™ 2
Stage 4 Winding Down the Estate™ 2
Stage 5 Petioning for the Final Order™ 2
Stage 6 Distribution and Discharge™ 3

STAGE 1
FILING A PETITION FOR PROBATE ™ 5
Key Components of Stage 1 Starting the Probate Case™ 5
   1. Gathering Information 5
   2. Document Preparation 6
   3. Petition Drafting 6
   3. Filing the Petition 6
   4. Setting the Court Hearing 6
Triggering Event for Moving to Stage 2: 7
What You Can Do Now, Even Before the Court Appoints
You As the Personal Representative 9
   1. Forward and Review the Decedent's Mail 9
   2. Notify Key Organizations and Institutions 10
   3. Utility and Service Notifications 10
   4. Additional Notifications 11
   5. Record Keeping 11
Your Responsibilities As the Personal Representative 11
   Understanding Your Fiduciary Duty 12
   Your Responsibilities Include 12
   Consequences of Non-Compliance 13

Scope of Legal Representation of You: What We Do Not Do .. 13
   1. Other Areas of Law 13
   2. Representation of the Estate 14
   3. Representation of Individuals 14
   4. Property and Tenancy Issues 14
   5. Handling of Assets 14
   6. Tax-Related Services 15
   7. Disputes Over Non-Probate Assets 15
Understanding the Probate Bond 15
   Purpose of a Probate Bond 15
   Determining the Bond Amount 16
   Cost of the Bond 16
   Options for Serving with a Probate Bond 16
   Process for Obtaining a Probate Bond 16
   Completion of Bond Obligation 17
Steps to Becoming the Personal Representative of an Estate .. 17
   Personal Representative Eligibility Requirements 17
   Filing the Petition 18
   Court Procedure 18
   Approval and Issuance of Letters 18
   Administration Authority 19

STAGE 2
APPOINTING THE PERSONAL REPRESENTATIVE™ 21
Stage 2 Appointing the Personal Representative™ 21
   1. Notice Requirements 21
   2. Preparation for the Court Hearing 21
   3. Court Hearing 22
   Triggering Event for Moving to Stage 3 22

STAGE 3
ESTATE ADMINISTRATION ™ 25
Key Components of Stage 3 25
   1. Asset Collection and Management 25
   2. Debt Settlement and Creditor Claims 25
   3. Tax Obligations 26
   4. Maintenance and Care of Estate Assets 26
   Triggering Event for Moving to Stage 4 26

Documentation Required for Estate Administration 28
- *Essential Documents* 28
- *Financial Documents*.. 28
- *Specific Asset Details* 28
- *Real Estate Transactions* 29
- *Expenses and Fees* 29

Guide to Administering the Estate as a Personal Representative 29
- *1. Gathering and Managing Assets*................................. 30
- *2. Selling Assets* 30
- *3. Dealing with Creditors*.. 30
- *4. Tax Responsibilities*... 30
- *5. Final Steps in Administration* 31

Locating the Decedent's Assets: A Guide for Personal Representatives 31
- *How We Can Help* 32
- *Your Responsibilities* 33
- *Additional Tips* 33
- *Inventory & Appraisal of Decedent's Assets*................... 34
- *Overview and Process* 34
- *What is an Inventory & Appraisal?*................................. 34
- *Why is it Necessary?* 34
- *Steps to Create an Inventory & Appraisal* 34
- *Common Delays*... 35
- *Your Role*... 36

Managing the Decedent's Real Estate: Your Options 36
- *1. Sell the Real Estate to a Third Party* 36
- *2. Purchase by You (as the Personal Representative)* 37
- *3. Purchase by an Heir*.. 37
- *4. Retention and Distribution to Heirs*........................... 37
- *Additional Considerations* 37

Detailed Process for Selling the Decedent's House to a Third Party or Heir... 38
- *1. Hiring a Real Estate Broker* 38
- *2. Listing the Property* 39
- *3. Accepting an Offer*.. 39
- *4. Opening Escrow* 39
- *5. Sending Notice of Proposed Action*............................ 39

  6. Court Confirmation of Sale 40
  7. Closing the Escrow 40
  Benefits of This Option 41
  Considerations.. 41
Options for the Personal Representative Buying the
Decedent's House 43
  Option #1: All Heirs Consent for You to Purchase
  the Real Estate 43
  Option #2: Court Confirmation of Sale 44
  Steps Involved in the Process 44
  Considerations..45
  Conclusion...45
Keeping the Decedent's House for Distribution to Heirs 47
  Distribution to Heirs 48
  Options to Cover Probate Costs and Fees............................48
  Considerations Before Deciding 49
Options to Remove an Occupant from the Decedent's
Real Estate 52
  1. Ask the Person Nicely to Move 53
  2. Offer Cash for Keys..53
  3. Eviction 53
  4. Probate Code Section 850 Petition 54
  Choosing the Right Approach 55
  Understanding the Need for Eviction..................................55
  Steps to Evict an Occupant 56
  Guidance on Handling Evictions... 57
  Why You Need Specialized Eviction Counsel 58
  Steps to Hiring an Eviction Attorney 58
  How We Can Assist 59
Managing Foreclosure on the Decedent's Property................59
  1. Sell the Real Estate..59
  2. Refinance the Real Estate...60
  3. Pay Off the Back-Payments..60
  Additional Considerations 61
Managing Potential Foreclosure of the Decedent's House...... 61
  1. Forward and Monitor the Decedent's Mail 61
  2. Identify Foreclosure Risks..62
  3. Communicate with the Foreclosure Trustee 62

 4. Notify the Estate's Attorney 62
 Legal Options to Address Foreclosure 63
 Obtaining a Temporary Restraining Order to Delay
 Foreclosure 64
 Conclusion 66
 Consequences of Not Properly Handling
 Foreclosure of the Decedent's House 66
 Steps to Avoid Negative Outcomes 67
 Conclusion 68
Managing Cash and Bank Accounts in the Decedent's Estate. 68
 Cash 68
 Checks 69
Opening an Estate Bank Account 69
 Using Estate Funds 70
 Record-Keeping 70
Handling Bank Accounts in the Decedent's Estate 70
 What We Need from You 71
 Steps to Follow 71
 Important Considerations 74
Appraising the Decedent's Tangible Personal Property 75
 Information Required for Appraisal 75
 Process for Appraisal 77
 Legal and Practical Considerations 78
 Understanding Specialty Appraisals in Estate
 Administration 79
Managing the Decedent's Tangible Personal Property 81
 Restrictions and General Guidelines 81
 Options for Disposing of Personal Property 82
 Steps Before Disposal 83
 Final Distribution 83
 Conclusion 84
Appraising the Decedent's Vehicle 84
 Information Required for Vehicle Appraisal 84
 Process for Appraisal 86
 Why Accurate Appraisal is Important 87
 Conclusion 87
Information Required for the Decedent's Mobile Home 87
 Essential Information for Mobile Home Appraisal 88

    Why This Information Is Necessary 89
    Steps to Follow 90
    Conclusion 91
Creating an Inventory and Appraisal for the Decedent's Brokerage Accounts 91
    Required Information for Each Brokerage Account 91
    Steps to Follow 92
    Legal and Financial Considerations 93
    Subpoena for Decedent's Brokerage Account Records 94
    Importance of Timely Information Collection 94
    Subpoena Process 94
    Costs and Fees 94
    Legal Considerations 95
    Steps Following Subpoena 95
    Communication 95
Giving Notice to Creditors in the Probate Process 96
    Steps to Identify and Notify Creditors 96
    Why Accurate Handling of Creditors is Important 99
    Conclusion 99
Dealing with Creditor Claims in the Probate Process 99
    Reviewing Creditor Claims 100
    Accepting or Rejecting Claims 100
    Legal Implications 101
    Conclusion 101
Filing the Decedent's Final U.S. Individual Income Tax Return (IRS Form 1040) 102
    Filing Requirements 102
    Tax Liabilities and Deductions 103
    Payment of Taxes 103
    Additional Considerations 103
    Documentation and IRS Communication 104
    Important Steps 105
    Closing Note 105
If It Is Taking More Than One Year for Estate Administration 105
    Requirements for Filing an Accounting or Status Report in Probate Cases 105
    Timeline for Closing a Probate Case 106

Filing Requirements After One Year 106
Role of Heirs 107
Consequences of Delay 108
Associated Costs 108
Final Steps 108
Summary 108
Ancillary Probate 109
Key Points of Ancillary Probate 109

STAGE 4
WINDING DOWN THE ESTATE ™ 113
Key Components of Stage 4 113
1. Final Accounting or Waiver Thereof 113
2. Drafting the Final Petition 114
3. Clearing Remaining Financial Obligations 114
Triggering Event for Moving to Stage 5 114
Winding Down the Estate After Administration Completion 116
Steps to Wind Down the Estate 117
After the Court Hearing 118
Conclusion 118
Understanding an Accounting in the Probate Process 119
Purpose of an Accounting 119
Components of an Accounting 119
Requirement for an Accounting 120
Filing an Accounting 120
Importance of Accuracy 120
Conclusion 120
Understanding a Waiver of Accounting in Probate 121
What is a Waiver of Accounting? 121
Process for Obtaining a Waiver of Accounting 121
Submissions to the Court Despite the Waiver 122
Legal Implications 122
Conclusion 123
Understanding Statutory Commission and Taxation of
Personal Representative Fees 123
Statutory Commission 123
Required Documentation for Accounting 123
Taxation of Personal Representative Fee 124

    Filing Requirements 124
    Conclusion... 125
Reimbursement for Administrative Expenses in Estate Administration 125
    What is Reimbursable? 125
    What is NOT Reimbursable?.. 126
    Requesting Reimbursement 127
    Importance of Compliance..127
Statutory Commissions for Ordinary Services....................... 128
    Calculating the Statutory Commissions 128
Extraordinary Fees for Extraordinary Services 129
    Definition and Examples of Extraordinary Services...... 130
    Approval and Payment of Extraordinary Fees 130
Deposit for Fees and Costs 131
    Here's what this entails 131
    Steps to File the Final Petition 132
Accounting or Waiver of Accounting 133
    Options for the Final Petition... 133
    Next Steps 134

STAGE 5
PETITIONING FOR THE FINAL ORDER 135
Key Components of Stage 5.. 135
    1. Notice of Hearing.. 135
    2. Addressing Probate Notes... 135
    3. Court Hearing... 136
    4. Judicial Approval and Final Order 136
Triggering Event for Moving to Stage 6 136
The Final Petition and Court Hearing.................................... 138
    Drafting and Filing the Final Petition 138
    Court Process 139
    Judge's Approval and Order... 139
    Final Steps of the Estate 139

STAGE 6
DISTRIBUTION AND DISCHARGE ™ 141
Key Components of Stage 6...141
    1. Distributing Assets..141

2. Handling Final Administrative Tasks 141
3. Ex Parte Petition for Final Discharge 142
4. Exonerating the Probate Bond 142
5. Resolving Remaining Funds 142
Completion of the Probate Process 143
Distribution and Final Discharge.. 145
Final Petition Approval and Order for Distribution 146
Verification of Amounts 146
Preparing for Distribution 146
Sending Distributions 146
Court Filing and Final Steps 146
Managing Reserve Funds 147
Threshold for Court Accounting 147

GLOSSARY OF COMMON PROBATE TERMS IN SIMPLE LANGUAGE.. 149

To Daba, You make me laugh and smile every day.
To Tippe, You make me strive to be a better person.
I love you both with all my heart.

ABOUT THE AUTHOR

R. Sam Price, J.D., LL.M.

R. Sam Price is not just a seasoned attorney; he's a trusted guide through the often complex world of estate planning, trust, and probate law. His knack for simplifying intricate legal language and procedures makes him a beacon for those navigating these challenging waters.

Expertise and Recognition

Sam is distinguished as a Certified Specialist in Estate Planning, Trust, and Probate Law by The State Bar of California Board of Legal Specialization. As the driving force behind Price Law Firm APC, he leads a dynamic team dedicated to providing top-notch legal services in estate planning, trust administration, and probate. His commitment to excellence extends beyond his practice as he chairs the San Bernardino County Bar Association Estate Planning and Probate Section. Here, Sam is instrumental in organizing monthly educational initiatives for peers and spearheading the annual Probate Symposium. Furthermore, his expertise and perspectives contribute significantly to the Executive Committee of the California Lawyers Association's Estates and Trusts Section, especially in legislative review and reporting.

Impact and Influence

Sam's prowess in representing clients in probate matters and his adeptness in handling both the prosecution and defense in probate and trust litigation have left lasting impressions. This impact was so profound that an author client immortalized him as a character in her novel "Battle of the Wills," a testament to his influence and dedication.

Educational Excellence

Sam's foundation in legal expertise is built upon a solid educational background. He embarked on his academic journey at California State University, San Bernardino, where he earned a bachelor's degree in Business Administration. This early exposure to business principles has informed his practical approach to estate planning. His academic achievements continued as he graduated with cum laude honors from Western New England College School of Law in Springfield, Massachusetts. Sam further distinguished himself in the legal field by earning a Master of Laws degree in Taxation from the prestigious New York University School of Law in New York, New York. This specialized education not only sharpened his skills but also positioned him as an authority in estate and tax planning law.

A Personal Touch

Beyond the courtroom and legal documents, Sam is a family man at heart. He cherishes moments with his wife Tiffany, a British TV reporter, their spirited seven-year-old son, and their beagle, Poppy. Sam's passion for the culinary arts sees him adventuring in the kitchen, where he delights in concocting new dishes.

In essence, Sam Price embodies not just legal acumen but a commitment to his clients' well-being, his family, and his community. He stands as a pillar of support, guidance, and innovation in estate planning and probate law.

THE 6-STAGE PROBATE PROCESS™

The 6-Stage Probate Process™ is designed as a structured framework to guide you through the probate process. It outlines the sequence of steps required at each stage and what must be accomplished to progress to the next phase. The process is linear, meaning once you complete the tasks of one stage and move to the next, there is no need to repeat the previous steps. Each stage is initiated by a specific triggering event that propels the case forward into the subsequent stage.

Detailed Breakdown of Each Stage

Stage 1 Starting the Probate Case™

- Objective: Gather necessary information and documents to prepare the Petition for Probate to request that a will be admitted to probate, if any, and to be appointed as the personal representative of the decedent's estate.
- Process: We gather information and documents to draft the Petition for Probate. Once the Petition for Probate is drafted, it is filed with the court.
- Triggering Event: Filing the Petition for Probate with the court and setting a court hearing date moves the case to Stage 2.

Stage 2 Appointing the Personal Representative™

- Objective: Execute the required public and personal notifications concerning the Petition for Probate, clear Probate Notes, and attend the court hearing.

- Process: This involves mailing notices, publishing details in a local newspaper, addressing any probate notes, and attending the scheduled court hearing.
- Triggering Event: The court's issuance of Letters of Administration or Letters Testamentary, empowering the representative legally, progresses the case to Stage 3.

Stage 3 Estate Administration™

- Objective: Marshal and manage the decedent's assets, and identify and pay creditors.
- Process: Collect assets, liquidate assets as necessary, settle debts with creditors, and file the decedent's final income tax returns.
- Triggering Event: Completion of these tasks allows the case to advance to Stage 4.

Stage 4 Winding Down the Estate™

- Objective: Gather information and documents to prepare the final petition that reports to the court the actions taken during the administration phase and an accounting, if necessary.
- Process: This petition may include a detailed accounting of the estate's transactions or a waiver of accounting if agreed by all heirs.
- Triggering Event: Filing of the Final Petition moves the case to Stage 5.

Stage 5 Petionting for the Final Order™

- Objective: Secure court approval of the final petition.
- Process: Notify interested parties of the hearing, resolve outstanding probate notes, and attend the court hearing.
- Triggering Event: The court's issuance of the Final Order transitions the case to the final stage.

Stage 6 Distribution and Discharge™

- Objective: Pay the administrative expenses and fees, distribute the estate's assets to the heirs and finalize the administrative responsibilities.
- Process: Pay any remaining administrative expenses, distribute assets or cash to heirs (who provide receipts), and handle any final obligations such as paying supplemental property taxes, filing the estate's income tax return or terminating the probate bond.
- Triggering Event: Filing an Ex Parte Petition for Final Discharge and receiving court approval for the same officially concludes the probate process.

This structured approach ensures that all legal requirements are met efficiently and provides a clear path from the initiation to the closure of the probate case. Each stage builds on the last, culminating in the orderly distribution of the decedent's assets and the formal discharge of the personal representative's duties.

The 6-Stage Probate Process ™
How to Navigate California Probate

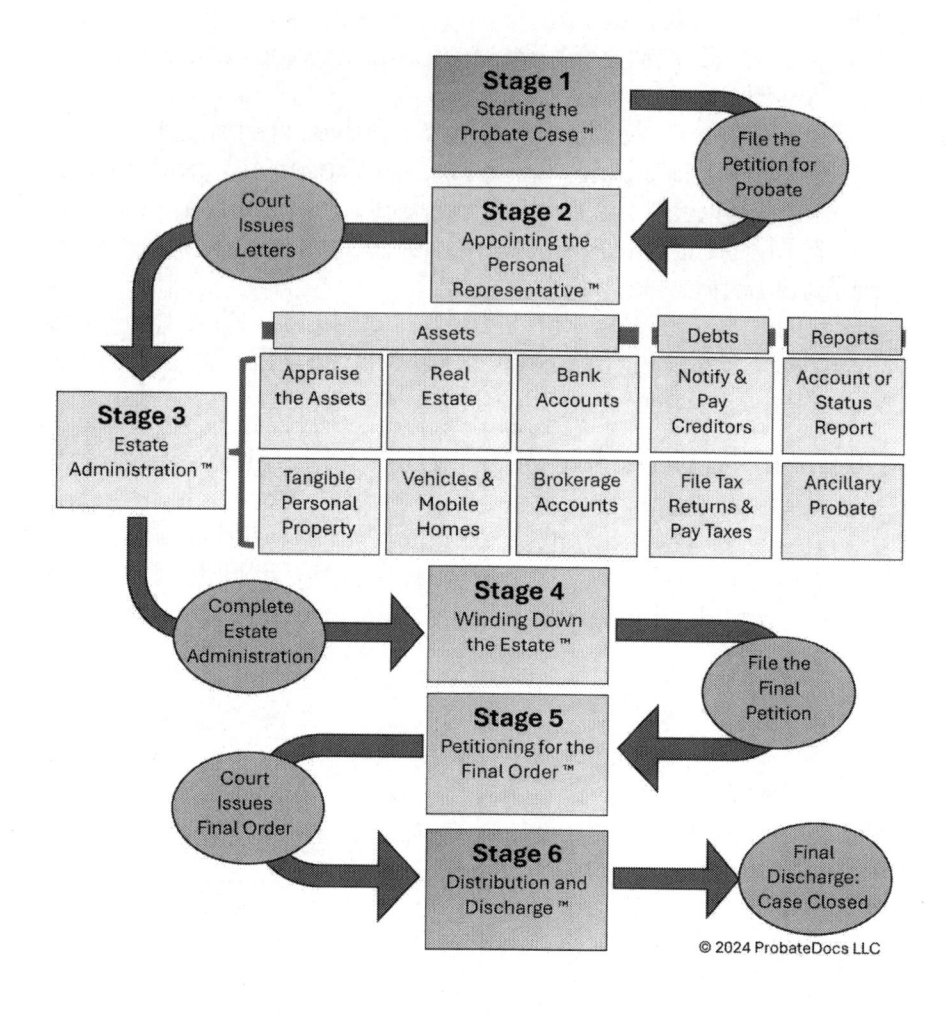

Stage 1 — Starting the Probate Case ™
- File the Petition for Probate

Stage 2 — Appointing the Personal Representative ™
- Court Issues Letters

Stage 3 — Estate Administration ™

Assets	Debts	Reports
Appraise the Assets	Notify & Pay Creditors	Account or Status Report
Real Estate	File Tax Returns & Pay Taxes	Ancillary Probate
Bank Accounts		
Tangible Personal Property		
Vehicles & Mobile Homes		
Brokerage Accounts		

Complete Estate Administration

Stage 4 — Winding Down the Estate ™
- File the Final Petition

Stage 5 — Petitioning for the Final Order ™
- Court Issues Final Order

Stage 6 — Distribution and Discharge ™
- Final Discharge: Case Closed

© 2024 ProbateDocs LLC

STAGE 1
FILING A PETITION FOR PROBATE ™

Stage 1: Starting the Probate Case™ is the foundational phase of the probate process, where the groundwork for the entire case is laid. This stage is crucial because it involves collecting all necessary information and documents required to draft and file the Petition for Probate. The effectiveness with which this stage is handled can significantly influence the efficiency of the entire probate process.

Key Components of Stage 1 Starting the Probate Case™

1. Gathering Information

- Decedent's Details: Obtain basic information about the decedent, including full name, date of birth, date of death, and last known address.
- Asset Documentation: Collect documents related to all assets, such as bank statements, stock certificates, real estate deeds, vehicle titles, and insurance policies.
- Debt Information: Gather information on any debts, including credit card statements, utility bills, mortgages, personal loans, and medical bills.

2. Document Preparation

- Death Certificate: Secure multiple certified copies of the death certificate, which will be required for various transactions throughout the probate process.
- Will Verification: If a will exists, verify its authenticity and understand its provisions. Determine the nominated executor and the beneficiaries listed.

3. Petition Drafting

- Draft the Petition for Probate based on the collected information. This document requests the court to officially appoint the executor (if there's a will) or an administrator (if no will exists) and to formally open the probate case.
- Petitioner signs the Petition for Probate verifying that the facts and true under penalty of perjury.

3. Filing the Petition

- Court Submission: File the completed Petition for Probate with the appropriate probate court. This submission must include all requisite forms and the original will (if one exists).
- Court Fees: Pay any required filing fees which can vary based on the jurisdiction and the complexity or value of the estate.

4. Setting the Court Hearing

- Court Scheduling: Once the petition is filed, the court will schedule a hearing date. This is typically set several weeks to months after filing, depending on the court's caseload and procedural timelines.
- Preparation for Hearing: Prepare for the initial probate hearing by ensuring all necessary parties are aware of the date and time, and by organizing any documents or information that may be needed to support the petition.

Triggering Event for Moving to Stage 2:

The triggering event that concludes Stage 1 and transitions the probate case to Stage 2 is the filing of the Petition for Probate with the court. This formal act sets the judicial process in motion by scheduling a court hearing and establishes the legal framework for administering the decedent's estate.

This stage is vital for setting a solid foundation for the probate process, ensuring all necessary legal thresholds are met, and preparing for the formal court proceedings that will officially start the administration of the estate.

- Legal Notices: Prepare to comply with legal requirements such as notifying potential heirs and beneficiaries and publishing notices in local newspapers, as mandated by law.

Stage 1: Starting the Probate Case ™

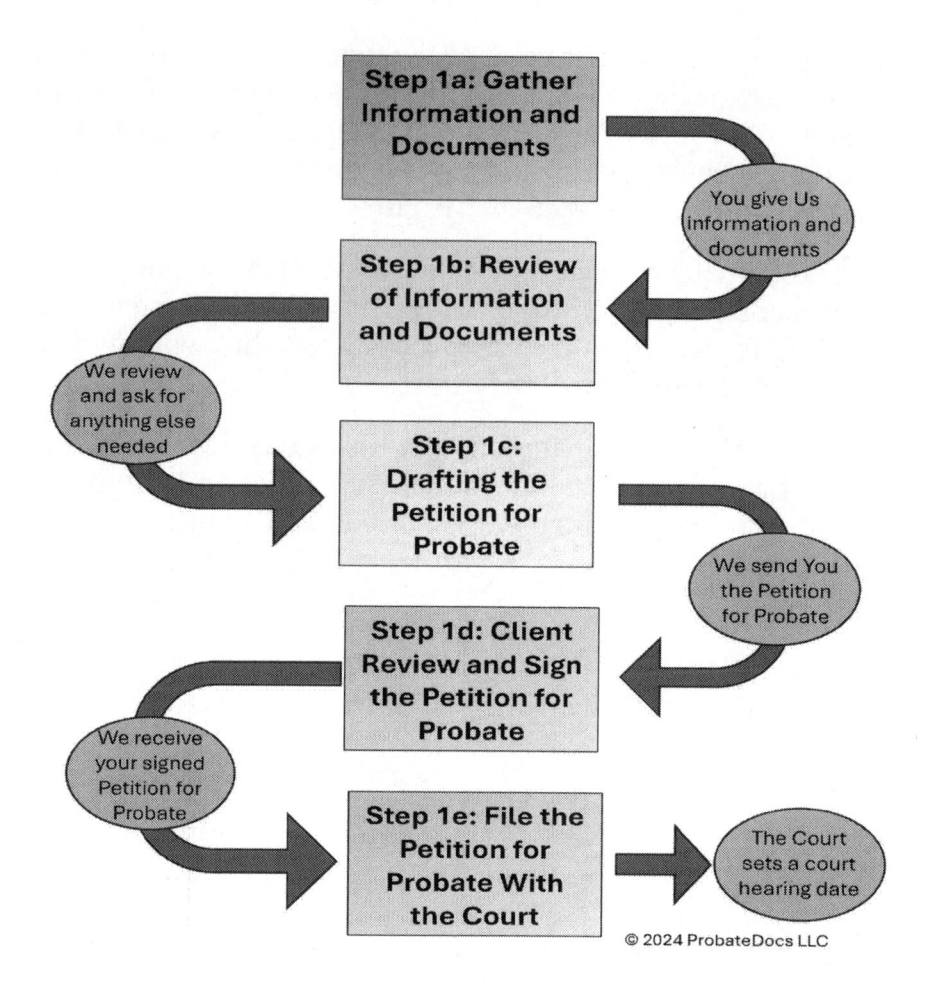

Step 1a: Gather Information and Documents

You give Us information and documents

Step 1b: Review of Information and Documents

We review and ask for anything else needed

Step 1c: Drafting the Petition for Probate

We send You the Petition for Probate

Step 1d: Client Review and Sign the Petition for Probate

We receive your signed Petition for Probate

Step 1e: File the Petition for Probate With the Court

The Court sets a court hearing date

© 2024 ProbateDocs LLC

Stage 1: Starting the Probate Case ™

Step	Tasks to Complete	What WE do	What YOU do	Estimated Time Frame
1a	Gather Information and Documents	We email You a Questionnaire to fill out electronically	You fill out the Questionnaire and email Us a copy of the Death Certificate, and the Will, if any. You overnight mail Us the original Will, if any	Within one business day of You signing the Retainer Agreement and paying a deposit
1b	Review of Information and Documents	We review the Questionnaire and documents, You provide information or documents needed	You respond with any information or documents, if needed	Time varies, with when You provide information and documents
1c	Drafting the Petition for Probate	We draft the Petition for Probate	You review and sign the Petition for Probate - Inform Us of any changes	Within three business days of having all information and documents needed
1d	Review and Sign the Petition for Probate	We email You the Petition for Probate to sign electronically		We will contact You when We send You the Petition for Probate to sign
1e	File the Petition for Probate with the Court	We file the Petition for Probate (We pay the court filing fee and eFiling fee from Your deposit)		Processing times may vary as the Court may take some time to process

© 2024 ProbateDocs LLC

What You Can Do Now, Even Before the Court Appoints You As the Personal Representative

Before you are officially appointed by the court, there are several proactive steps you can take to manage the decedent's affairs effectively. This initial period is critical, as it helps ensure that the estate is protected and that all legal and financial obligations are addressed promptly. Here's a guide to help you navigate this process:

1. Forward and Review the Decedent's Mail

Ensure you forward all mail to your address. This is vital as it will keep you informed about any ongoing financial obligations, upcoming deadlines, or issues that need immediate attention. Open and read the mail regularly to track any correspondence from creditors, financial institutions, or other important parties.

2. Notify Key Organizations and Institutions

- Creditors: Inform any known creditors of the decedent's passing as soon as possible to discuss the state of any debts.
- Foreclosure Notices: If you receive any notices such as a Notice of Default or Notice of Trustee Sale, inform your attorney immediately to address any potential risk to the decedent's property.
- Banks and Brokerage Firms: Provide copies of recent bank and brokerage statements to your attorney to help them understand the decedent's financial position.
- Insurance: Confirm that there is active insurance on the decedent's house and vehicles. Check when these policies expire, and if the house is now vacant, notify the insurance company, as standard homeowners insurance may not cover a vacant property after the owner's death.
- Health, Life, and Other Insurances: Notify these companies to cancel policies and refund any unused premiums. This includes health insurance and possibly life insurance if applicable.

3. Utility and Service Notifications

- Social Security Administration: Contact at (800) 772-1213 to report the death. Be aware of the need to repay any payments issued after the death date.
- Veterans Administration: If the decedent was a veteran, notify them at (800) 698-2411 to handle benefits and other related matters.
- Utilities: Notify utility companies to cease services unless necessary to maintain the property in good condition.

4. Additional Notifications

- Banks: Inform the decedent's banks to freeze accounts to prevent any unauthorized transactions. Remember that automatic mortgage payments will also stop, so alternate arrangements may need to be made.
- Credit Card Companies and Employers: Notify these to close accounts or to claim any unpaid benefits, such as salary, vacation time, or death benefits.
- Landlords: If the decedent was renting, notify the landlord. The lease terms might dictate the estate's responsibilities.
- Subscription Services: Cancel any ongoing subscriptions like newspapers or magazines.

5. Record Keeping

Keep detailed records of all notifications and correspondences. These records will be invaluable for legal and tax purposes and will help ensure that no part of the estate management process is overlooked.

By taking these steps, you can protect the estate and ensure that everything is in order for when you are officially appointed by the court. If you encounter any difficulties or require further advice during this process, do not hesitate to contact your attorney for guidance.

Your Responsibilities As the Personal Representative

As the personal representative of an estate, you take on a crucial role with significant responsibilities. Your duties are outlined under the law to ensure that the estate is managed and distributed fairly and responsibly, not just to the heirs but also to any creditors. This role requires a high level of diligence and integrity, as it is guided by what is known as a fiduciary duty—the highest standard of care established by law.

Understanding Your Fiduciary Duty

As a fiduciary, you must prioritize the interests of the estate's creditors and heirs above your own. This duty ensures that all actions taken are in the best interests of those who have stakes in the estate.

Your Responsibilities Include

- Acting in the Best Interest of the Estate: Always make decisions that benefit the creditors and heirs, even if they conflict with your personal interests.
- Keeping Stakeholders Informed: Regularly update the creditors and heirs about the estate's proceedings and any significant developments.
- Prudent Management of Assets: Handle the estate's investments wisely, aiming to preserve or increase the estate's value while avoiding unnecessary risks.
- Asset Identification and Protection: Locate all assets of the estate and take steps to secure and maintain them.
- Notification to Creditors: Notify all known or reasonably ascertainable creditors of the estate, inviting them to submit their claims according to the law.
- Separation of Assets: Keep the estate's funds and other assets separate from your personal assets to avoid any mix-up or mismanagement.
- Banking Responsibilities: Deposit the estate's cash in interest-bearing accounts at a recognized California bank.
- Inventory and Appraisal: Compile a detailed inventory of the estate's assets and file an appraisal with the court within four months of your appointment.
- Record-Keeping: Maintain meticulous records and accounts of all transactions, expenses, and management activities related to the estate.
- Communication with Legal Counsel: Stay in regular contact with your attorney to discuss the estate and inform them promptly of any changes in your contact information or significant circumstances affecting the estate.

Consequences of Non-Compliance

Failing to meet these responsibilities can have serious repercussions. The court has the authority to impose penalties, including:

- Financial Penalties: Fines or reduction of your compensation.
- Removal: Termination of your role as the personal representative.
- Liability for Debts: Personal liability for the estate's debts if mismanagement is proven.
- Other Sanctions: Various other penalties that the court deems necessary to enforce compliance and protect the estate's interests.

Your role as the personal representative is pivotal. It requires a thoughtful, organized approach to ensure that the estate is handled correctly and lawfully. Always consider seeking advice from your attorney to navigate the complexities of probate law effectively.

Scope of Legal Representation of You: What We Do Not Do

In our role as your attorneys, it's important to clarify the scope of our services to ensure you understand what we can and cannot do for you as part of our representation. Our services are specialized and focused on probate and estate planning, and there are certain legal matters that fall outside of our practice area or role. Here's an outline of what we do not do:

1. Other Areas of Law

- Non-Probate Legal Matters: We specialize exclusively in probate and estate planning. This means we do not handle legal issues that fall outside these areas, such as criminal defense, personal injury, or family law.

2. Representation of the Estate

- Estate as a Separate Entity: The estate itself is not considered a separate legal entity that can have its own attorney. We represent you in your capacity as the personal representative of the estate, not the estate itself.

3. Representation of Individuals

- Role as an Heir: While we represent you as the personal representative, we do not represent you in your potentially different role as an heir to the estate.
- Other Heirs: We do not represent any other heirs of the estate, nor can we provide legal advice to any of them. Our legal duties are to you alone as our client.

4. Property and Tenancy Issues

- Evictions: Our practice does not cover landlord-tenant law, including evicting individuals from estate properties. For such matters, it will be necessary to consult with an attorney who specializes in this area.
- Real Estate Transactions: We do not engage in selling real estate properties. You will need to work with a licensed real estate broker to list and sell any real property belonging to the estate.

5. Handling of Assets

- Asset Collection: We do not physically collect or handle estate assets. Our role is to provide legal guidance on how assets should be managed and distributed according to probate laws.

6. Tax-Related Services

- Tax Preparation and Filing: We do not prepare or file tax returns for the estate. You should consult with a qualified tax professional for these services.

7. Disputes Over Non-Probate Assets

- Non-Probate Disputes: Some assets may not pass through probate (e.g., those held in a trust or with designated beneficiaries). We do not handle disputes related to such non-probate assets.

Understanding these boundaries will help ensure that your expectations align with the services we can provide, and will also guide you in seeking additional professional advice when necessary. If you have any questions or need referrals to other specialists, please feel free to ask.

Understanding the Probate Bond

A probate bond serves a crucial role in the administration of an estate. It acts like an insurance policy that safeguards the interests of creditors and heirs by ensuring proper management and completion of the probate process. Here's a breakdown of what a probate bond is and how it functions within the probate system:

Purpose of a Probate Bond

The probate bond ensures that:

1. Funds are Available: It provides a financial guarantee that there will be sufficient funds to cover all probate-related costs and debts.
2. Heirs Receive Their Inheritance: It secures the assets to be distributed to heirs in accordance with the decedent's wishes.

3. Completion of Probate: It obligates you, as the personal representative, to faithfully execute the duties required throughout the probate process.

Determining the Bond Amount

The amount required for the probate bond typically depends on the value of the estate's assets. The larger the estate, the higher the bond amount might be.

Cost of the Bond

The annual premium for the probate bond is influenced by your creditworthiness and financial stability. This premium must be paid yearly as long as the bond is in effect.

Options for Serving with a Probate Bond

- Full Probate Bond: This is generally the standard requirement unless specified otherwise.
- Minimum Probate Bond: You might qualify for a reduced bond if the will waives the need for a bond or all heirs agree to waive it. Nevertheless, you must fully disclose the estate's debts and your efforts to locate all creditors to the court.
- No Probate Bond: In rare cases, no bond is required if all conditions for a waiver are met and documented in court. This option is seldom approved without clear waivers from the will and all heirs.

Process for Obtaining a Probate Bond

1. Application: You'll fill out a bond application, and we will submit it on your behalf.

2. Payment: If approved, you are responsible for the initial

premium, which may be paid out of your pocket or from the estate's funds if available.

3. Annual Renewal: Each year, you will receive an invoice from the bond company. The premium should ideally be paid from the estate's funds, but if insufficient funds are available, you may need to cover the cost personally.

Completion of Bond Obligation

The obligation to maintain the probate bond continues until all estate distributions are complete and the court processes the Ex Parte Petition for Final Discharge. This closure can take several months, during which you are still responsible for the bond premium.

It's important to understand that failure to pay the bond premium can lead to serious consequences, including legal action against you by the bond company. If you have any questions about the probate bond or need assistance with the application process, please feel free to contact our office.

Steps to Becoming the Personal Representative of an Estate

As you consider taking on the role of personal representative for an estate, it's important to understand the requirements and the process involved. Below is an outline of what you need to know and the steps we will take to assist you in being appointed by the court.

Personal Representative Eligibility Requirements

To petition the court to become the personal representative of an estate, you must meet the following criteria:

- Age: You must be over eighteen years old.

- Residency: You must live in the United States.
- Acceptance of Responsibilities: You must be willing to accept the duties and responsibilities that come with being the personal representative.

Filing the Petition

Once we gather all necessary information and documents from you, we will prepare and file a petition with the probate court. This petition requests that the court appoint you as the personal representative of the estate.

Court Procedure

- Court Hearing: After filing the petition, the court will schedule a hearing. While your presence at the hearing is not mandatory, you are welcome to attend. We will represent you at the hearing.
- Notices: Prior to the court hearing, we are required to send notices to all interested parties, including heirs and other potential claimants, informing them of the petition. Additionally, we will publish a notice in a local newspaper to inform the broader community and potential creditors.
- Probate Notes: The court might have questions or require further information about the petition, often referred to as probate notes. We may need to respond in writing, or in some cases, amend the petition. We might contact you to gather more information or to have you sign additional documents as needed.

Approval and Issuance of Letters

- Order for Probate: If your petition is successful and no significant objections are raised, the court will issue an Order for Probate during the hearing, formally appointing you as the personal representative.
- Issuance of Letters: "Letters" are official documents issued

by the court that authorize you to act as the personal representative. If a probate bond is required, the court will issue the Letters after the bond has been filed.

Administration Authority

Once you receive the Letters, you will have the legal authority to administer the estate, which includes managing assets, paying debts, and eventually distributing the assets to the rightful heirs according to the will or state law if there is no will.

We will guide you through each step of this process, ensuring that you are fully prepared for your responsibilities as a personal representative. If you have any questions or need further clarification, please do not hesitate to contact us.

STAGE 2
APPOINTING THE PERSONAL REPRESENTATIVE™

Stage 2: Appointing the Personal Representative™ marks a critical transition in the probate process, moving from the initial setup and petition to actively engaging in the probate proceedings to secure the legal authority to act on behalf of the decedent's estate. This stage culminates with the court's issuance of Letters of Administration or Letters Testamentary, which formally authorize the personal representative to begin estate administration duties.

Stage 2 Appointing the Personal Representative™

1. Notice Requirements

- Mailing Notices: Send notices of the probate hearing to all interested parties, including heirs, beneficiaries, and any others who may have a legal interest in the estate. This ensures that all potential stakeholders are informed and have the opportunity to participate or object during the probate proceedings.
- Publication: Publish a notice of the petition in a local newspaper as required by law. This serves to inform potential creditors and other interested parties who might not be reached by direct mailing.

2. Preparation for the Court Hearing

- Addressing Probate Notes: Probate courts often issue "probate notes" – queries or requests for additional information or

clarification on the petition filed. Addressing these notes promptly and accurately is crucial to avoiding delays in the appointment process.
- Gathering Documentation: Organize and prepare all documentation that supports the petition and addresses any issues raised in the probate notes. This may include further verification of the will's validity, documentation of assets, or additional details on the heirs.

3. Court Hearing

- Attending the Hearing: The personal representative, typically represented by their attorney, must attend the court hearing. During this session, the judge reviews the petition, hears any objections, and assesses the overall readiness of the petitioner to serve as the personal representative.
- Court Decision: If the court is satisfied with the information presented and no valid objections are raised, it will issue Letters of Administration (if there is no will) or Letters Testamentary (if there is a will). These documents grant the petitioner the authority to act as the personal representative of the estate.

Triggering Event for Moving to Stage 3

The issuance of Letters of Administration or Letters Testamentary by the court is the triggering event that concludes Stage 2. Receiving these letters signifies that the court has formally recognized the petitioner as the personal representative, granting them the legal authority to manage the decedent's estate. This authority is crucial for undertaking all subsequent actions required to administer and ultimately close the estate.

This stage is critical as it involves significant interaction with the court system and requires meticulous attention to procedural details to ensure that the personal representative is duly appointed without delays. The successful conclusion of this stage sets the stage for the comprehensive management of the estate, including asset gathering, creditor payment, and eventual distribution to heirs.

Stage 2: Appointing the Personal Representative ™

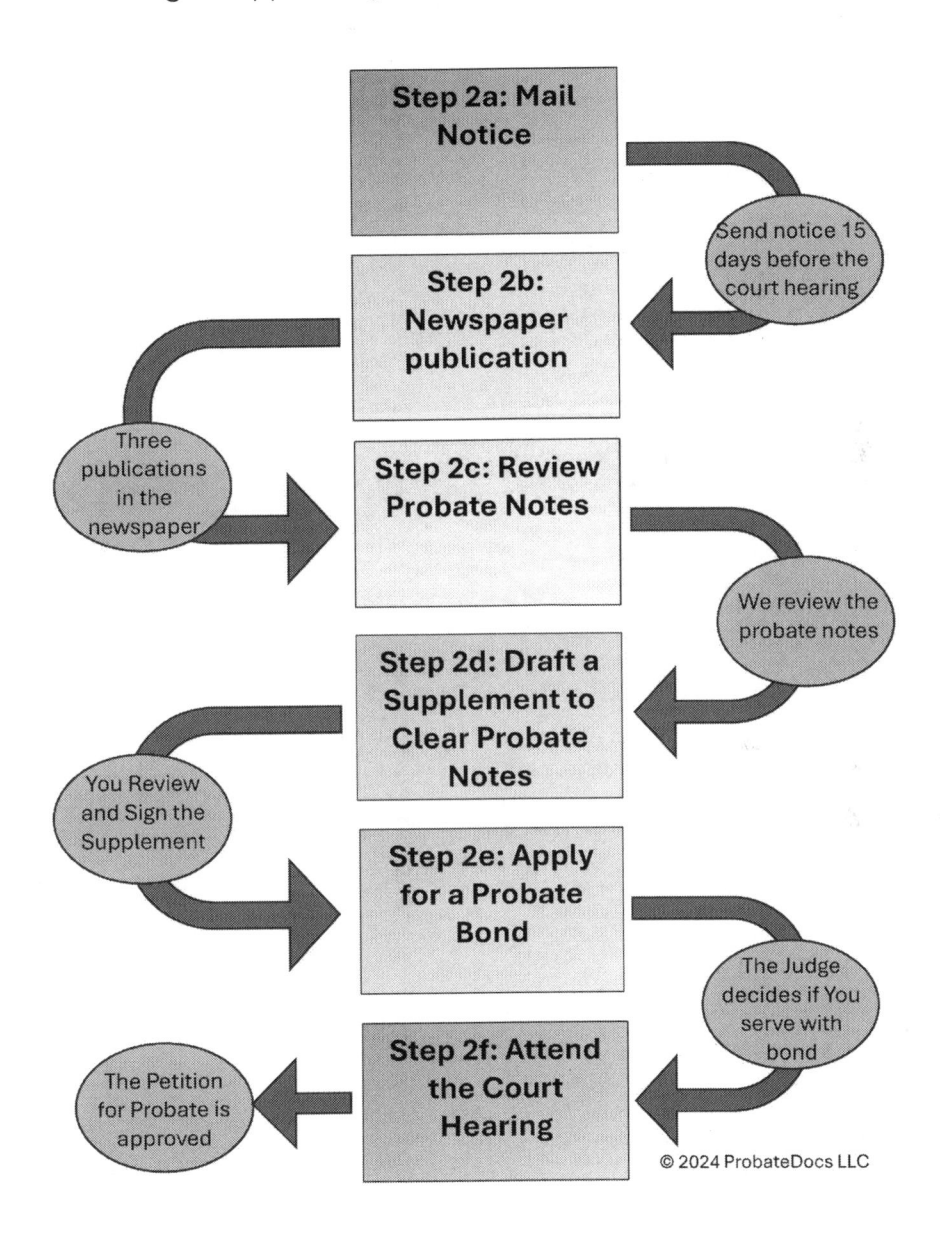

Step 2a: Mail Notice
- Send notice 15 days before the court hearing

Step 2b: Newspaper publication
- Three publications in the newspaper

Step 2c: Review Probate Notes
- We review the probate notes

Step 2d: Draft a Supplement to Clear Probate Notes
- You Review and Sign the Supplement

Step 2e: Apply for a Probate Bond
- The Judge decides if You serve with bond

Step 2f: Attend the Court Hearing
- The Petition for Probate is approved

© 2024 ProbateDocs LLC

Stage 2: Appointing the Personal Representative ™

Step	Tasks to Complete	What WE do	What YOU do	Estimated Time Frame
2a	Mail Notice	We mail a notice of the Petition for Probate to all persons entitled to notice (We pay the eFiling fee from Your deposit)		Mailed at least 15 days before the court hearing
2b	Newspaper Publication	We publish notice in a newspaper (We pay for the publication from Your deposit)		The first of three publications is at least 15 days before the court hearing
2c	Review Probate Notes	We review the court's Probate Notes, and ask You for any additional information or documents needed	You respond with any needed information or documents	Time varies, with complexity of Your case and when You gather information and documents
2d	Draft a Supplement to Clear Probate Notes	We draft a Supplement to clear the Probate Notes (We pay the eFiling fee from Your deposit)	You review and sign the Supplement - Inform Us of any changes	Completed within two business days once we have Your information and documents
2e	Probate Bond	We apply for the Probate Bond (We pay for the first annual premium from Your deposit)	You sign the bond with an original signature (not electronic)	Time varies, depending on the bond company processing time
2f	Court Hearing	We attend the court hearing	You don't have to attend the court hearing, but You can attend if You want to	Our hearing will be very short, but We may have to wait for other hearings

© 2024 ProbateDocs LLC

STAGE 3
ESTATE ADMINISTRATION ™

Stage 3: Estate Administration™ is the core phase of the probate process where the personal representative, now formally authorized by the court, actively manages the decedent's estate. This stage involves consolidating assets, addressing debts and taxes, and preparing the estate for eventual distribution.

Key Components of Stage 3

1. Asset Collection and Management

- Identifying and Gathering Assets: The personal representative compiles a comprehensive list of the decedent's assets, which can include bank accounts, securities, real estate, personal property, and business interests. Each asset must be secured and evaluated for its current value.
- Appraisal of Assets: Certain assets, particularly real estate and unique personal items, may require professional appraisal to determine their fair market value for both tax assessment and equitable distribution purposes.

2. Debt Settlement and Creditor Claims

- Notification to Creditors: The personal representative must notify known and unknown creditors of the estate proceedings, typically through direct notifications and public notices. This allows creditors to file claims for debts owed by the decedent.
- Evaluating Creditor Claims: Each claim must be assessed for its validity and relevance to the estate. Valid claims are

paid out of the estate's assets, while dubious claims may be contested or rejected, subject to legal guidelines.

3. Tax Obligations

- Filing Decedent's Final Income Tax Returns: The personal representative is responsible for filing any outstanding income tax returns on behalf of the decedent, covering the period up to the date of death.
- Handling Estate Taxes: If the estate exceeds certain thresholds, it may be liable for federal and/or state estate taxes. Preparing these tax returns can be complex and often requires professional assistance.

4. Maintenance and Care of Estate Assets

- Upkeep of Property: Real estate and other tangible assets must be maintained in good condition to preserve their value. This includes paying ongoing expenses such as property taxes, utilities, and insurance.
- Managing Investments: For estates that include investment portfolios or business interests, the personal representative must manage or oversee these assets prudently, often with the help of financial advisors or managers.

Triggering Event for Moving to Stage 4

The completion of asset consolidation, debt resolution, and tax filings marks the end of the active administration phase. Once these tasks are accomplished, the personal representative is ready to prepare for the final stages of the probate process.

Moving to Stage 4 - Winding Down the Estate™ involves transitioning from managing the estate to preparing and filing the final documents with the court. This includes drafting a final petition that outlines all actions taken and proposing how the remaining assets should be distributed to the heirs. This stage typically culminates in the personal representative seeking the court's approval to distribute the assets and close the estate.

Estate administration is the most labor-intensive part of the probate process, requiring meticulous attention to detail and strict adherence to legal and financial obligations. Successful completion of this stage sets the groundwork for the final settlement and distribution of the estate.

Stage 3A: Inventory and Appraisal ™

Step	Tasks to Complete	What WE do	What YOU do	Estimated Time Frame
3A1	Gather Information and Documents	We email You a Questionnaire to fill out electronically	You fill out the Questionnaire and email documents to Us	After the Court issues Letters to You
3A2	Review of Information and Documents	We review the Questionnaire and documents, You provide information or documents needed	You respond with any information or documents, if needed	Time varies, with complexity of Your case and when You gather information and documents
3A3	Drafting the Petition for Probate	We draft the Inventory and Appraisal and Property Tax Certificate	You review and sign the Inventory and Appraisal	Within three business days of having all information and documents needed
3A4	The Probate Referee Appraisal	We send the Inventory and Appraisal to the Probate Referee (We pay the appraisal fee from Your deposit)		The Probate Referee can take up to 60 days to complete the Inventory and Appraisal
3A5	Mailing the Inventory and Appraisal	We mail the Inventory and Appraisal to Everyone		Within 3 business days of receiving the Inventory and Appraisal
3A6	File the Inventory and Appraisal with the Court	We file the Inventory and Appraisal with the Court - (We pay the eFiling fee from Your deposit)		Processing times may vary as the Court may take some time to process

© 2024 ProbateDocs LLC

Documentation Required for Estate Administration

As we prepare to administer the estate, it's essential to gather all necessary documentation to ensure a smooth and effective process. Here is a detailed list of documents and information we will need from you:

Essential Documents

1. Death Certificate: A certified copy of the decedent's death certificate is required to prove the date and fact of death.
2. Original Will: If the decedent left a will, please provide the original document as it is necessary for the probate proceedings.

Financial Documents

3. Bank Statements: We need all bank statements from the decedent's accounts starting from the date of death until the funds are withdrawn. Additionally, once you open an estate bank account, please provide these statements as well.
4. Asset List: A comprehensive list of all assets within the estate. This includes but is not limited to real estate, vehicles, stocks, bonds, and personal items.

Specific Asset Details

5. Vehicles: For each vehicle, provide the year, make, model, mileage, condition, and either the registration, title document, or any document containing the VIN number.
6. Investments: For stocks, bonds, and mutual funds, provide statements as of the date of death, along with the ticker symbol, CUSIP number, and the number of shares.
7. Firearms: List each firearm by make, type, and serial number.

Real Estate Transactions

8. Real Estate Documentation: If a house or any other property is being sold, provide the contact details of your real estate broker, the listing agreement, the purchase agreement, the contact details of your escrow officer, and the escrow closing statement.

Expenses and Fees

9. Funeral Expenses: Submit any receipts or invoices for funeral expenses or any other funds you have advanced on behalf of the estate that you wish to be reimbursed for.

10. Extraordinary Fees: If you seek compensation for extraordinary services performed for the estate, provide a detailed report including the date, description, and time spent on these tasks.

These documents are critical for us to accurately assess the estate's value, fulfill legal requirements, and effectively manage and distribute the estate's assets. Ensuring all paperwork is complete and submitted in a timely manner will help avoid delays in the probate process. If you have any questions or need assistance in gathering these documents, please do not hesitate to contact our office.

Guide to Administering the Estate as a Personal Representative

Once you are appointed as the personal representative and receive your "letters" of administration, you gain the authority to manage and settle the estate of the decedent. Administering an estate involves several key responsibilities and tasks that must be conducted meticulously to ensure the estate is handled according to the law and the wishes of the decedent. Here is an overview of the primary duties involved in this process:

1. Gathering and Managing Assets

- Identifying Assets: Locate all assets of the estate, such as bank accounts, stocks, bonds, real estate, and personal property.
- Securing Assets: Open a bank or brokerage account in your name as the personal representative to consolidate and manage the estate's liquid assets safely.

2. Selling Assets

- Real Estate and Other Valuables: If necessary, sell the decedent's real estate and other valuable assets. This is often required to liquidate assets to pay creditors and distribute the inheritance to heirs.

3. Dealing with Creditors

- Notice to Creditors: Provide formal notice to all known and ascertainable creditors of the estate. This involves reviewing the decedent's mail and other records to identify any outstanding debts.
- Evaluating Claims: Review and approve or reject creditor claims. Make arrangements to pay valid debts from the estate's funds.

4. Tax Responsibilities

- Filing Tax Returns: You are responsible for filing any outstanding federal and state income tax returns the decedent did not file. Additionally, file a final income tax return covering the period from January 1 to the date of death.
- Paying Taxes: Ensure that all due taxes, along with any interest and penalties, are paid by the estate.

5. Final Steps in Administration

- Preparing for Closure: You can begin winding down the estate at least four months after receiving your letters, but all tasks must be completed to proceed with closing the estate.
- Filing a Final Petition: Gather all necessary documents and information to file a final petition with the court. This petition is essential for formally concluding the probate process.
- Paying Probate Costs: Ensure that all costs related to the probate process are paid.
- Distributing Remaining Assets: After all debts and expenses are settled, distribute the remaining assets to the heirs according to the will or state law.
- Filing Receipts: Provide the court with receipts and other documentation proving that all assets have been properly distributed.
- Requesting Discharge: File an ex parte petition for final discharge to officially conclude your role as personal representative.
- Exonerating the Bond: If a probate bond was posted, take steps to have it exonerated, releasing you from further obligations under the bond.

Throughout this process, it is crucial to keep detailed records of all actions and transactions. This documentation will be vital for court proceedings and for maintaining transparency with the heirs and creditors. If you have any questions or require assistance during this process, do not hesitate to reach out to our office. We are here to support you every step of the way in your duties as a personal representative.

Locating the Decedent's Assets: A Guide for Personal Representatives

As the personal representative of an estate, one of your primary responsibilities is to locate all assets belonging to the decedent. This can be a complex task, especially if the decedent had a variety of assets distributed in different places. Below, we outline how we can assist you in this search and what you will need to do on your end.

How We Can Help

1. VEHICLES

- California DMV Search: We can assist you in searching for any vehicles registered to the decedent through the California Department of Motor Vehicles. This will reveal any vehicles owned by the decedent in California.

2. UNCLAIMED PROPERTY

- California Database Search: We can search California databases for any unclaimed property the decedent may have. For this, please provide us with every city in California where the decedent lived. If we find unclaimed property, you will need to apply to receive these funds on behalf of the estate.

3. INSURANCE POLICIES AND ANNUITIES

- Nationwide Database Search: We can request a search in a nationwide database of insurance companies to find any insurance policies or annuities the decedent had. This search can take four to six months. The benefits will go directly to any named beneficiaries. If no beneficiary is named, these may become assets of the probate estate.

4. REAL ESTATE

- Public Records Search: We can conduct a search for any real estate owned by the decedent in California. This search is done county-by-county based on the counties you provide where the decedent may have owned property. We are unable to search for real estate properties outside California.

Your Responsibilities

1. Personal Documents and Correspondence

- Mail and Financial Statements: Review the decedent's mail for any bank statements, financial statements, or correspondence that might indicate asset ownership.

2. Financial Institutions

- Bank Accounts: Identify and contact any banks where the decedent had accounts.
- Brokerage Accounts: Locate any financial institutions where the decedent had brokerage accounts.
- Retirement Accounts: Check for any retirement accounts the decedent had with various financial institutions.

Additional Tips

- Safe Deposit Boxes: If the decedent had a safe deposit box, you will need to access it to check for any important documents or valuables.
- Personal Records: Examine personal records, tax returns, and other documents that might indicate asset ownership or debts.

These steps will help you form a comprehensive picture of the decedent's assets, which is crucial for proper estate administration. If you encounter any difficulties or have questions about the process, please reach out to our office for guidance. We are here to assist you through every step of this important responsibility.

Inventory & Appraisal of Decedent's Assets

Overview and Process

The process of inventory and appraisal (I&A) is a critical step in the administration of an estate. It involves creating a detailed list of the decedent's assets and determining their value at the time of the decedent's death. This serves as the foundation for preparing tax returns and for the final accounting that must be filed with the court.

What is an Inventory & Appraisal?

An Inventory & Appraisal is essentially a catalog of the decedent's assets, which includes everything from bank accounts to personal property, along with their appraised values. This document is crucial for accurately reporting the estate to the court and relevant tax authorities.

Why is it Necessary?

The I&A allows the court and the heirs to understand the extent and value of the estate. It is used to ensure that taxes and debts are properly paid and that the distribution of the estate's assets to the heirs is based on the actual values of those assets.

Steps to Create an Inventory & Appraisal

1. Gathering Information:

- You, as the personal representative, are responsible for collecting all necessary documentation related to the decedent's assets. This may include bank statements, brokerage statements, real estate deeds, and other relevant financial documents.
- If there are difficulties in obtaining certain documents, such

as bank statements, we may assist by issuing subpoenas to obtain these records.

2. Drafting the Inventory & Appraisal:

- Our team will draft the I&A based on the information you provide. This draft will list all known assets and their estimated values at the time of the decedent's death.

3. Signing the Inventory & Appraisal:

- Once the draft is complete, you will need to review and sign the document, confirming that all information is accurate and complete to the best of your knowledge.

4. Appraisal by the Probate Referee:

- The signed I&A is then sent to a Probate Referee, appointed by the court, who will officially appraise the assets. The Probate Referee's role is to provide an independent valuation of the estate's assets.

5. Distribution and Filing:

- After the appraisal, the I&A is mailed out to all heirs of the estate, providing them with a transparent view of the asset valuations.
- Finally, the completed I&A is filed with the court within the required timeframe, typically within four months from the date the Letters of Administration were issued to you.

Common Delays

- Bank and Financial Statements: Obtaining these documents is often the biggest delay in the process. It's important to act quickly to request and gather all necessary financial records.
- Asset Appraisal: The appraisal process can also introduce delays, especially if the Probate Referee is handling multiple cases. Recently, appraisals have been taking up to two months.

Your Role

As the personal representative, your prompt and diligent collection of asset information is crucial. The sooner you can gather and provide all required details, the smoother the process will be. Delays in providing information can lead to missed deadlines and prolonged probate proceedings.

Please make sure to stay proactive and organized in gathering the necessary documents and information. If you encounter any challenges or have questions during this process, do not hesitate to reach out to us for assistance.

Managing the Decedent's Real Estate: Your Options

As the personal representative of the estate, you have several options when it comes to handling the decedent's real estate. These options can affect the overall administration of the estate, the timing of asset distribution, and potentially the financial outcome for the heirs. Below are the primary options available to you regarding the decedent's house:

1. Sell the Real Estate to a Third Party

- Overview: This option involves selling the property on the open market. It can help in settling the estate's debts and distributing the net proceeds among the heirs as per the will or intestacy laws.
- Process: The house will be listed for sale, typically through a real estate agent. After the sale, the proceeds, after paying off any associated debts and costs (like mortgages, liens, and real estate commissions), will be added to the estate's assets for distribution.

2. Purchase by You (as the Personal Representative)

- Overview: If you are also an heir or interested party, you may opt to buy the property yourself.
- Considerations: This option requires transparency and often an independent appraisal to ensure the sale price is fair to all parties, especially if other heirs are involved. It's important that this transaction is handled like any arm's length transaction to avoid conflicts or claims of impropriety.

3. Purchase by an Heir

- Overview: Similar to the previous option, another heir may wish to purchase the property.
- Process: The heir interested in purchasing the property must agree to buy it at a price deemed fair and reasonable, which often requires an independent appraisal. The transaction should be treated as if the heir were a third party to ensure fairness to all heirs.

4. Retention and Distribution to Heirs

- Overview: The estate holds onto the property until the conclusion of the probate process, after which it is transferred to one or more heirs according to the decedent's will or state law.
- Considerations: This option may be chosen if the property is meant to remain within the family or if selling the property is not financially prudent at the time of probate. This choice might involve additional costs for upkeep and taxes during the probate process, which the estate must manage.

Additional Considerations

- Legal and Tax Implications: Each option comes with specific legal and tax implications. For instance, selling the property

may have capital gains tax implications, whereas transferring it might affect the estate's liquidity.
- Market Conditions: Real estate market conditions can significantly impact the best choice. It might be advantageous to sell during a high market and disadvantageous during a downturn.
- Estate's Financial Needs: The decision may also depend on the estate's need to liquidate assets to cover debts and expenses.

It's important to consult with estate professionals, such as your attorney and a tax advisor, to understand the full implications of each option. This will help ensure that your decision aligns with both the estate's needs and the best interests of the heirs. If you have any questions or need further advice on how to proceed with the real estate, please feel free to contact us.

Detailed Process for Selling the Decedent's House to a Third Party or Heir

Selling real estate from an estate is a common method to liquidate a significant asset and use the proceeds for paying debts, taxes, and eventually distributing the remainder to the heirs. Here's a step-by-step guide to help you understand the process of selling the decedent's house to a third party or heir:

1. Hiring a Real Estate Broker

- Selection: You must choose a reputable real estate broker experienced in handling estate sales. The broker will be responsible for assessing the property, suggesting any necessary repairs or improvements, and determining the market value to set a competitive selling price.
- Contract: Engaging a broker typically involves signing a listing agreement, which authorizes the broker to list, market, and handle the sale of the property on behalf of the estate.

2. Listing the Property

- Market Analysis: The broker will perform a comparative market analysis to suggest a listing price based on similar properties recently sold in the area.
- Marketing: The property will be marketed through various channels, including online real estate platforms, local listings, and the broker's network to attract potential buyers.

3. Accepting an Offer

- Offer Review: You will review purchase offers submitted by interested parties. This involves considering the terms of each offer, including the purchase price, contingencies, and the buyer's financial qualifications.
- Negotiation: You may negotiate the terms of the offer to ensure the best possible outcome for the estate.

4. Opening Escrow

- Escrow Account: Once an offer is accepted, an escrow account will be opened to securely hold the buyer's deposit and facilitate the transaction. The escrow agent will ensure that all parts of the sale are completed according to the contractual terms before any money changes hands.

5. Sending Notice of Proposed Action

- Notice Requirements: If you were appointed as the personal representative with full authority under the Independent Administration of Estates Act (IAEA), we will send out a Notice of Proposed Action to all interested parties, typically heirs or beneficiaries. This notice includes details of the sale and offers a 15-day waiting period during which recipients can object to the terms of the sale.
- Waiting Period: If no objections are received within the waiting

period, the sale can proceed. If there are objections, these must be resolved before moving forward.
- However, if anyone has objected to the sale, then to sell under to the current buyer under the current terms, we must petition the court to confirm the sale.

6. Court Confirmation of Sale

- Petitioning the Court to Approve the Sale: If you were appointed with limited authority under the IAEA, or if anyone objected to the Notice of Proposed Action, then we must petition the court to confirm the sale. This involves publishing a notice in the newspaper to advertise the sale, filing a petition with the court, posting a notice at the courthouse, mailing written notice to all persons entitled to notice, and attending a court hearing.
- Auction at the Court Hearing: At the court hearing, the judge acts as the auctioneer and anyone who is qualified can bid on the property. There are detailed rules of qualifying to bid and how much the initial bid must be. The judge accepts the highest bidder.
- Confirming the Sale: At the court hearing, the judge will confirm the sale to the original buyer, or to an over-bidder. With that court order confirming the sale, the escrow can proceed to close.

7. Closing the Escrow

- Finalizing the Sale: Once all conditions of the sale are met (e.g., inspections, financing, and compliance with local regulations), the escrow will close. This involves signing final documents, transferring the property title to the buyer, and disbursing funds.
- Disbursement: After paying off any mortgages or liens against the property, the remaining funds are added to the estate's assets for eventual distribution.

Benefits of This Option

- Liquidity: Selling the property converts it into cash, which can be easier to distribute among multiple heirs and useful for settling the estate's debts.
- Efficiency: A sale handled through a broker and escrow can often be completed more efficiently than transferring property to heirs, especially if the property would need to be sold by the heirs later.

Considerations

- Costs: Remember to account for costs such as broker's fees, escrow fees, and any taxes or legal fees associated with the sale.
- Market Conditions: The real estate market can significantly influence the timing and financial outcome of the sale.

This comprehensive process ensures that the sale of the property is handled professionally and in compliance with legal standards, helping to protect the estate's assets and the interests of its beneficiaries. If you have any questions about this process or need assistance with any steps, feel free to contact our office for guidance.

Probate Sale of Real Estate to a Third Party or Heir

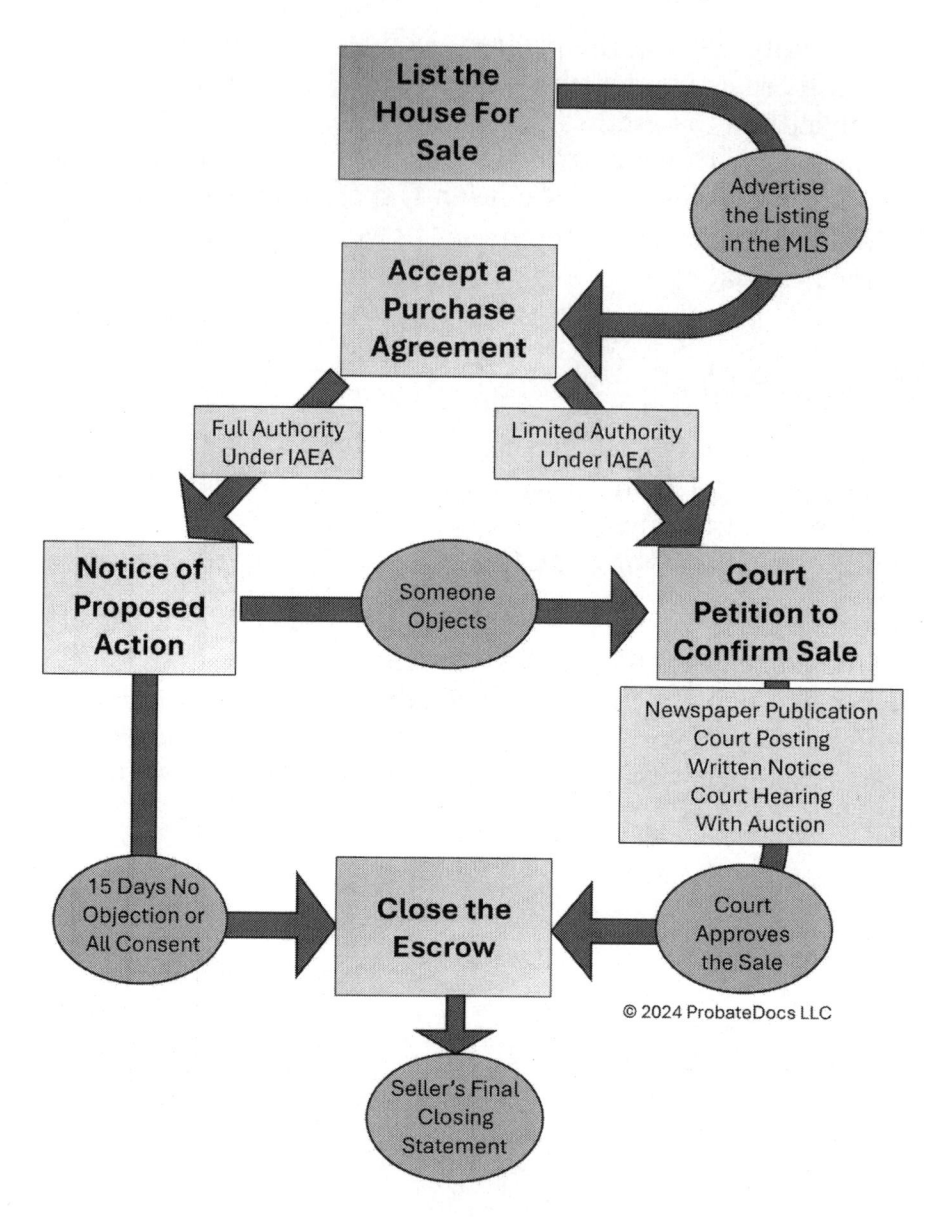

- **List the House For Sale**
  - Advertise the Listing in the MLS
- **Accept a Purchase Agreement**
  - Full Authority Under IAEA → **Notice of Proposed Action**
  - Limited Authority Under IAEA → **Court Petition to Confirm Sale**
- Someone Objects (Notice of Proposed Action → Court Petition to Confirm Sale)
- Court Petition to Confirm Sale:
  - Newspaper Publication
  - Court Posting
  - Written Notice
  - Court Hearing With Auction
- 15 Days No Objection or All Consent → **Close the Escrow**
- Court Approves the Sale → **Close the Escrow**
- Seller's Final Closing Statement

© 2024 ProbateDocs LLC

Stage 3B: Sell the House to a Third-Party or Heir ™

Step	Tasks to Complete	What WE do	What YOU do	Estimated Time Frame
3B1	List the House for Sale	We can refer You to a real estate broker that knows probate, if needed	You sign a listing agreement with a real estate broker, and put Us in email contact	As soon as the Court issues Letters to You
3B2	Accept an Offer to Purchase		You accept an offer to purchase by signing the purchase agreement	Time varies with how quickly the offers come in on the house
3B3	Notice of Proposed Action	We draft a Notice of Proposed Action (NOPA) with the Purchase Agreement to notify everyone that there is a sale of the home (We pay the eFiling fee from Your deposit)		Within one business day of receiving the signed Purchase Agreement; 15-day objection period
3B4	Court Confirmation of Sale, if Required	We draft the Court Confirmation of Sale, if needed – We file with the Court (We pay the court filing fee and the eFiling fee from Your deposit)	You sign the Court Confirmation of Sale	Completed within two business days once we have Your information and documents
3B5	Close the Escrow	We send Escrow the NOPA and a letter stating that they are clear to close	You sign the escrow instructions and ancillary documents, You send Us the final closing statement	Typically 30 – 45 days from the opening of escrow

© 2024 ProbateDocs LLC

Options for the Personal Representative Buying the Decedent's House

As the personal representative of an estate, if you are considering purchasing real estate owned by the estate, there are specific legal procedures that must be followed to ensure transparency and fairness to all parties involved, especially the heirs of the estate. Here are the options available to you:

Option #1: All Heirs Consent for You to Purchase the Real Estate

1. Heir Consent: Obtain consent from all heirs of the estate. This is the simplest method where all heirs agree in writing that they are comfortable with you purchasing the property.
2. Court Approval: Even with full heir consent, the purchase requires court approval to ensure the sale price is fair and

that the interests of all parties, including creditors of the estate, are protected.
3. Filing a Petition: We will prepare and file a petition with the probate court to seek approval for your purchase of the property. This petition will include the terms of the sale and the appraisal to justify the proposed purchase price.
4. Appraisal: An appraisal of the property must be conducted within the past year to establish the property's market value. This ensures that the transaction is conducted at a fair market price, safeguarding the estate's and heirs' interests.

Option #2: Court Confirmation of Sale

1. *Petition for Court Confirmation*: If not all heirs consent to the sale or if you prefer this route for any reason, a petition must be filed seeking court confirmation of the sale. This process includes additional safeguards.
2. *Deposit and Terms*: You will need to make a 10% deposit of the offered purchase price. The terms of the sale, including the deposit amount, will be detailed in the petition filed with the court.
3. *Court Hearing and Auction*: The court will set a hearing date, and there will be a public auction at the hearing. The property is open to bids from other interested parties, not just from you. This ensures that the estate has the opportunity to receive the highest possible price.
4. *Overbidding Process*: During the court hearing, other potential buyers can place higher bids (overbids) than your initial offer. You will have the opportunity to match or exceed these bids if you wish to proceed with purchasing the property.

Steps Involved in the Process

- Preparation: Gathering all necessary documents, including the latest appraisal and proposed terms of sale.
- Filing: Submitting the necessary legal documents and petitions to the court.

- Notification: Notifying all interested parties, including all heirs and potential creditors, about the sale and the court hearing.
- Court Hearing: Attending the court hearing, where the judge will review the sale's terms and conduct the auction if necessary.

Considerations

- Transparency: This process is designed to be transparent to protect the estate's and heirs' interests and ensure you are paying a fair price for the property.
- Legal Compliance: It is crucial to comply with all legal requirements to avoid any conflicts of interest or legal challenges to the sale.

If you decide to pursue purchasing the decedent's house, we will guide you through every step of these options, ensuring that all legal requirements are met and that the process is handled smoothly and transparently. If you have any questions or need further clarification, please do not hesitate to reach out.

Conclusion

Purchasing the entire property from an estate can be a significant transaction requiring careful legal consideration. Whether through mutual agreement among the heirs or a court-supervised process, it's crucial to ensure that all legal steps are followed meticulously to safeguard your rights and those of other stakeholders in the estate. If you decide to move forward with purchasing the decedent's house, we will provide full support and guidance throughout the process.

Probate Sale of Real Estate to the Personal Representative

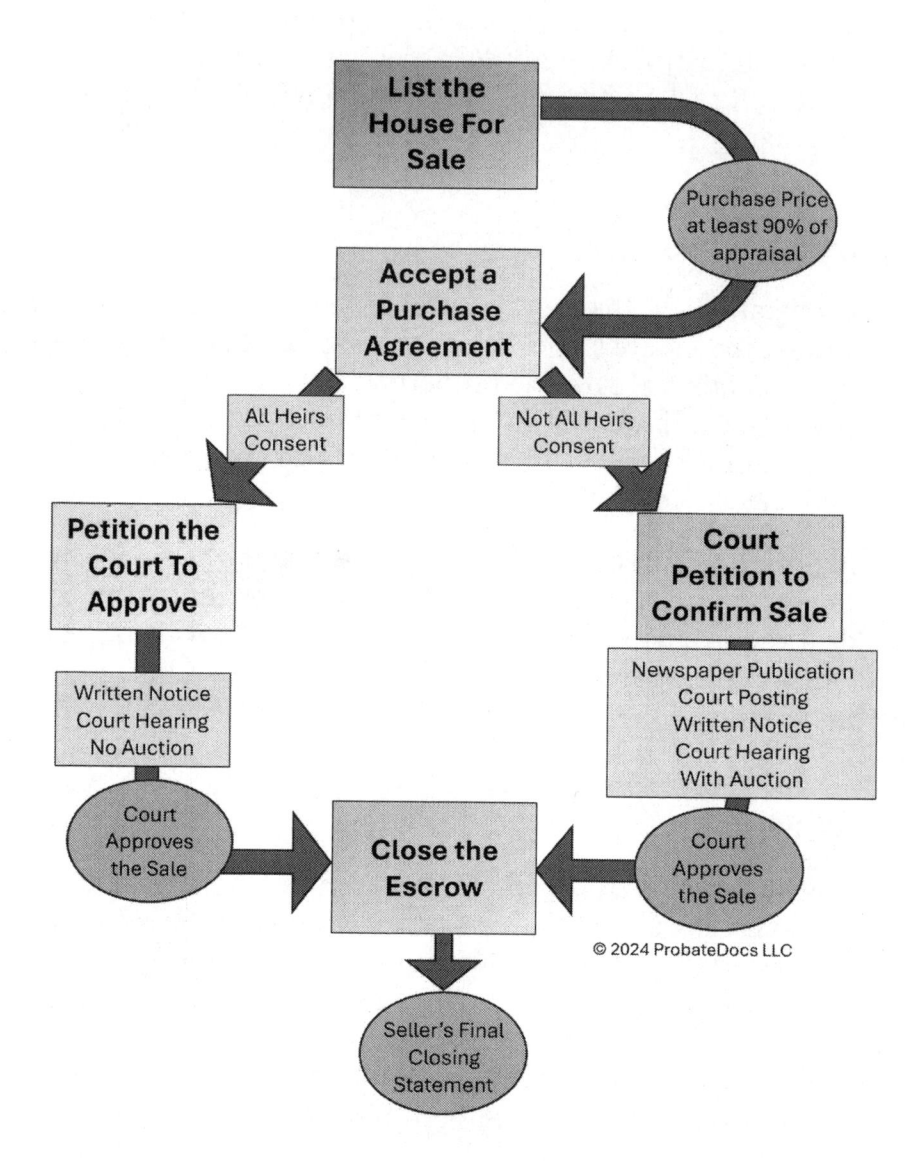

List the House For Sale

Purchase Price at least 90% of appraisal

Accept a Purchase Agreement

- All Heirs Consent
- Not All Heirs Consent

Petition the Court To Approve

Written Notice
Court Hearing
No Auction

Court Approves the Sale

Court Petition to Confirm Sale

Newspaper Publication
Court Posting
Written Notice
Court Hearing
With Auction

Court Approves the Sale

Close the Escrow

Seller's Final Closing Statement

© 2024 ProbateDocs LLC

Stage 3B: You Buy the House ™

Step	Tasks to Complete	What WE do	What YOU do	Estimated Time Frame
3B1	Hire a Real Estate Broker and Get Qualified for a Loan	We can refer You to a real estate broker that knows probate, if needed	You sign a listing agreement with a real estate broker, and put Us in email contact	As soon as the Court issues Letters to You
3B2	Accept a Purchase Agreement		You get qualified for financing and sign the purchase agreement	Time varies with how quickly the offers come in on the house
3B3	Notice of Proposed Action	We draft a Notice of Proposed Action (NOPA) with the Purchase Agreement for Everyone to consent	You talk with all the heirs to get their consent to You buying the house at the purchase price	Within one business day of receiving the signed Purchase Agreement; Everyone must sign the consent to the purchase
3B4	Option 1: Court Confirmation of Sale	We draft the Court Confirmation of Sale – Auction at the Court Hearing (We file & pay with Your deposit)	You sign the Court Confirmation of Sale	Completed within three business days once we have Your information and documents, Court Hearing date varies
3B5	Option 2: Petition for Court Approval	We draft a Petition for Court Approval if Everyone consents – No Auction at the Court Hearing (We file & pay with Your deposit)	You sign the Petition for Court Approval	Completed within three business days once we have Your information and documents, Court Hearing date varies
3B6	Close the Escrow	We send Escrow the NOPA, Court Order, and a letter stating that they are clear to close (We pay the eFiling fee from Your deposit)	You sign the escrow instructions and ancillary documents	Typically 30 – 90 days from the opening of escrow

© 2024 ProbateDocs LLC

Keeping the Decedent's House for Distribution to Heirs

Choosing to retain the decedent's real estate and distribute it to the heirs at the conclusion of the probate process is a significant decision that can affect how the estate is settled. Here are the key aspects and options for managing the costs associated with keeping the property within the estate until the case is resolved.

Distribution to Heirs

- Joint Ownership: Upon completion of the probate case, the real estate can be transferred to the heirs as per the decedent's will or, in the absence of a will, according to state intestacy laws. This means that all designated heirs will receive a portion of the property, which they will co-own.
- Considerations: Co-ownership can sometimes lead to complications, especially if the heirs have different ideas about what to do with the property. It is essential to discuss and possibly reach an agreement on how to manage or eventually dispose of the property.
- Distribution In-Kind of Property and of Cash: Rather than owning the real estate jointly between all the heirs, one heir may want to keep the house while others may want to receive cash for their inheritance. This is more common than joint ownership. To be fair, the equity of the real estate at the time of distribution should equal the cash to the other heirs of the estate, and all of the heirs must consent to this option and how much they will receive.

Options to Cover Probate Costs and Fees

Managing the costs and fees associated with probate while retaining the property requires careful financial planning. Here are some options:

1. PAY OUT-OF-POCKET:

- Description: One or more heirs might choose to cover the probate costs and any ongoing expenses related to the property (like taxes, maintenance, insurance) out-of-pocket. This is straightforward but requires sufficient personal financial resources.
- Advantages: Avoids additional debt or encumbrances on the property.
- Disadvantages: Can be financially burdensome for the heirs.

2. GET A LOAN AGAINST THE PROPERTY:

- During Probate: The Personal Representative can apply for a loan secured against the real estate to cover probate expenses and any cash going to the other heirs. This option is useful if the estate lacks sufficient liquid assets to cover these costs and cash inheritance. The loan is a temporary loan, just long enough to get the probate case completed and paid for.
- Refinancing After Probate: Once probate is complete and the heirs officially own the property, they must refinance the property to pay off the initial temporary probate loan.
- Considerations: Loans increase the financial risk, including the potential for foreclosure if the loan payments are not made. It's crucial to assess the loan terms carefully. This will add more complexity to your case, and it is sometimes difficult to get everyone to agree to this procedure.

3. USE ESTATE'S CASH:

- Description: If the estate has enough liquid assets, these can be used to pay probate costs, legal fees, and other related expenses.
- Advantages: Utilizing the estate's cash reserves can prevent the need for loans or personal outlays by the heirs.
- Disadvantages: This might reduce the cash available for distribution among heirs.

Considerations Before Deciding

- Long-Term Financial Impact: Assess the long-term financial implications of retaining the property, including potential appreciation or depreciation, and the costs of upkeep.
- Heirs' Agreement: It is advisable for all heirs to agree on a plan for managing the property post-probate to avoid future conflicts.
- Legal and Tax Advice: Consult with a probate attorney and

a tax advisor to understand all legal ramifications and tax implications of retaining real estate in an estate.

By carefully considering these options and implications, heirs can make informed decisions that align with their financial capabilities and the wishes of the decedent. If you have any questions or need further assistance with planning or decision-making regarding the estate's real estate, please do not hesitate to contact our office.

Options for Keeping the Real Estate

Options to Distribute the House In-Kind

Option 1: Distribute the House In-Kind to All Heirs

Option 2: Distribute the House In-Kind to One Heir and Cash to Others

Options To Pay Probate Costs and Cash Inheritance

Option 1: The Estate Has Enough Cash to Pay	Option 2: The Heirs Pay Out-of-Pocket	Option 3: The Personal Representative Gets a Loan Against the House
The Estate's cash is sufficient to pay all the Probate Costs and any cash inheritance. Everyone must consent to what they receive. All heirs receive their full inheritance either in cash or in-kind.	The Heirs pay for the Probate Costs and any cash inheritance out of their own personal funds. Everyone must consent to what they receive. All heirs receive their full inheritance either in cash or in-kind.	The Personal Representative borrows against the house to pay the Probate Costs and any cash inheritance. Everyone must consent to what they receive. All heirs receive their full inheritance either in cash or in-kind. The house must be refinanced after distribution in-kind.

© 2024 ProbateDocs LLC

Stage 3B: Keep the House: Distribute In-Kind ™

Step	Tasks to Complete	What WE do	What YOU do	Estimated Time Frame
3B1	Decide to Keep the House	We will explain Your options to keep the house and make an in-kind distribution of the house to the heirs	You inform Us of your decision to keep the house and make an in-kind distribution of the house to the heirs	As soon as the Court issues Letters to You
3B2	Cash in the Estate	We draft a Proposed Estimated Distribution to estimate the costs and fees	The estate has enough cash to pay the costs and fees of the probate case.	Time varies with how quickly estate administration is completed
3B3	Get a Loan	We put you in contact with a Loan Officer to get a temporary loan on the house to pay the fees and costs of probate	You get a temporary loan on the house during the probate case to pay the costs and fees; You refinance with a permanent loan after the probate case is over	Loan is closed within 30 – 45 days
3B4	You Pay From Your Own Funds	We draft a Proposed Estimated Distribution to estimate the costs and fees	You pay for the costs and fees of the probate case out of Your own funds	Time varies with how quickly estate administration is completed
3B5	Some Heirs Get House and Others Get Cash	We estimate how much cash to some heirs and house to other heirs, We draft a NOPA for Everyone to consent (We pay the eFiling fee from Your deposit)	You talk to the heirs for them to consent	Time varies with how quickly estate administration is completed

© 2024 ProbateDocs LLC

Options to Remove an Occupant from the Decedent's Real Estate

As the personal representative, you may encounter situations where it's necessary to remove an occupant from the decedent's property. Here are the various strategies you can consider, each with its own legal and practical considerations:

1. Ask the Person Nicely to Move

- Approach: A simple and direct approach can sometimes resolve the issue without legal proceedings. You might explain the situation regarding the estate's requirements and ask the occupant to vacate voluntarily.
- Advantages: This method avoids legal costs and the stress associated with formal eviction proceedings.
- Disadvantages: If the occupant refuses to leave, further action will be necessary.

2. Offer Cash for Keys

- Explanation: This approach involves offering the occupant a sum of money in exchange for vacating the property and handing over the keys. This agreement should be formalized in writing.
- Process: Determine an appropriate amount that is agreeable to both parties. Draft and both parties sign a written agreement that specifies the terms of the move-out, including the move-out date and the condition in which the property should be left.
- Advantages: Often quicker than eviction, reduces potential damage to the property, and avoids legal proceedings.
- Disadvantages: There is a cost involved, which the estate must bear.

3. Eviction

- Legal Process: If the occupant refuses to leave voluntarily or through cash for keys, you may need to initiate formal eviction proceedings.
- Steps:

1. Notice to Vacate: Serve the occupant with a legal notice to vacate, specifying the reason for eviction and the time frame they have to leave.
2. File an Eviction Lawsuit: If the occupant does not comply with the notice, file an eviction lawsuit in your local court.

3. Court Hearing and Order: Present your case in court. If the judge rules in your favor, you will receive a court order for eviction.

- Advantages: Legally enforceable method to remove an occupant.
- Disadvantages: Can be time-consuming, costly, and potentially contentious.

4. Probate Code Section 850 Petition

- Explanation: A Section 850 Petition, often referred to as a "petition to determine title," can be filed in probate court to resolve issues concerning property claimed to belong to the estate but is held by someone else.
- Use Case: This is particularly useful if the occupant claims some right to the property or if there is a dispute over the property's ownership.
- Process:

1. File the Petition: Submit a petition under Probate Code Section 850 asking the court to determine the rightful ownership of the property.
2. Legal Proceedings: The court will schedule hearings to review claims and evidence from both sides.
3. Court Decision: The court will issue a ruling that may include ordering the occupant to vacate if their claim is unsubstantiated.

- Advantages: Resolves ownership disputes legally; clear, court-ordered solutions.
- Disadvantages: Can be lengthy and requires legal representation.

Choosing the Right Approach

- Consider the Relationship: If the occupant is a family member or close to the decedent, more sensitive handling may be appropriate.
- Evaluate the Estate's Position: Assess the financial implications of each option. For instance, cash for keys might be more expedient but also involves upfront costs.
- Legal Guidance: Consult with a probate or real estate attorney to ensure that whichever method you choose complies with local laws and effectively protects the estate's interests.

Each option should be carefully considered based on the specific circumstances surrounding the estate and the occupant's situation. If you need further guidance on these options or assistance with the process, please contact our office. Evicting an Occupant from the Decedent's House

As the personal representative of the estate, managing the decedent's property includes dealing with occupants who may be residing in the estate's real estate without a legal right or after their legal right has expired. Here are the options available for evicting an occupant from the house:

Understanding the Need for Eviction

- Unlawful Occupants: These might be tenants who have overstayed their lease terms, individuals who moved in without any formal agreement, or family members who do not have a legal right to reside in the property.
- Legal Heirs or Beneficiaries: If the legal heirs or beneficiaries are occupying the property and need to be evicted, the process may be more sensitive and will require careful legal handling.

Steps to Evict an Occupant

1. *Legal Assessment:*

- Determine Status: First, ascertain the legal status of the occupant. Are they a tenant with a lease, a relative, a friend, or someone else? This will determine the legal approach required.
- Review Lease Agreements: If the occupant is a tenant under a lease, you will need to review the lease terms to confirm whether they are in violation of the lease or if the lease has expired.

2. *Communication:*

- Notice to Vacate: Generally, you should start by providing a written notice to vacate the property. The duration of the notice period may vary depending on the local landlord-tenant laws.
- Negotiation: It may be beneficial to negotiate with the occupant to vacate voluntarily, which can save time, legal expenses, and potential distress.

3. *Legal Action:*

- Filing an Eviction: If the occupant does not comply with the notice to vacate, you may need to file an eviction lawsuit in the local court. This is particularly necessary if dealing with tenants legally bound by a lease agreement.
- Court Process: The eviction process will involve court hearings where you must present a valid reason for eviction, such as the end of a lease term, violation of lease conditions, or the need to liquidate the property as part of settling the estate.

4. Handling Post-Eviction:

- Regaining Possession: Once the eviction is granted by the court, law enforcement may assist in regaining possession of the property if the occupant refuses to leave voluntarily.
- Property Management: After eviction, ensure the property is secured, maintained, and prepared for sale or transfer according to the estate's plans.

Legal Considerations

- Compliance with Laws: Ensure that all actions comply with local and state eviction laws, which vary significantly from one jurisdiction to another.
- Representation: It may be advisable to hire an attorney who specializes in real estate or landlord-tenant law to handle the eviction process, especially to ensure that the rights of the estate and the legal process are properly managed.

Costs

- Eviction Costs: Be prepared for the costs associated with filing an eviction, including court fees, attorney fees, and potential costs for securing the property post-eviction.

Evicting an occupant from estate property must be handled with legal care to avoid violating tenant rights and to ensure the process aligns with the estate's best interests. If you encounter issues with occupants in the decedent's property or need assistance navigating the eviction process, please contact our office for further guidance and support.

Guidance on Handling Evictions

As your probate attorney, I want to ensure that you are well-informed and supported in managing all aspects of the estate. However, it's important to note that our legal practice is specialized in probate and estate planning, and we do not handle eviction cases directly. Evictions, especially those involving unlawful detainer actions, require specialized legal expertise in landlord-tenant law.

Why You Need Specialized Eviction Counsel

1. Expertise in Landlord-Tenant Law: Eviction processes are governed by specific laws that vary significantly from state to state and even between local jurisdictions. Attorneys specializing in evictions have the necessary knowledge and experience to navigate these laws effectively.
2. Proper Representation: An eviction attorney will be able to represent the estate's interests in court, ensuring that all legal protocols are followed and that the estate's rights are vigorously defended.
3. Avoiding Legal Pitfalls: Improperly handled evictions can lead to delays, additional expenses, and potential legal liabilities for the estate. An experienced eviction lawyer will help avoid these pitfalls.

Steps to Hiring an Eviction Attorney

- Research: Look for attorneys or law firms that specialize in landlord-tenant disputes or specifically in evictions. You may want to consult legal directories or seek recommendations from other professionals.
- Consultation: Schedule consultations with potential attorneys to discuss the specific situation, their approach to handling evictions, and their fees. It's important to feel confident in the attorney's ability to handle the matter efficiently and effectively.
- Engagement: Once you decide on an attorney, you will need to formally engage their services, typically by signing a retainer agreement. This document will outline the terms of your working relationship, including their fees and the services they will provide.

How We Can Assist

While we do not handle evictions directly, we are committed to supporting you through the process by:

- Providing Documentation: Supplying any necessary documents from the estate that may be required for the eviction proceedings, such as proof of ownership, the will, and any relevant communications with the occupant.
- Coordination: Working with your eviction attorney to ensure they have a full understanding of the estate's circumstances and how the eviction fits into the broader context of estate administration.
- Advice on Estate Matters: Offering guidance on how the eviction may impact other aspects of the estate administration, including timing and financial considerations.

It's important to handle this matter with the appropriate legal support to ensure it is resolved in a manner that protects the estate's interests. If you need recommendations for qualified eviction attorneys or have any further questions on how this process impacts the estate, please do not hesitate to reach out to our office. We are here to assist you throughout the administration of the estate.

Managing Foreclosure on the Decedent's Property

If the decedent's house is in foreclosure or at risk of foreclosure, it's crucial to understand the available options to address this situation effectively. As the personal representative, you have several strategies to consider to either resolve the foreclosure or mitigate its impact on the estate. Here are your options:

1. Sell the Real Estate

- Quick Sale: Selling the property can be a viable option to pay off the mortgage and avoid foreclosure. This might be the best

choice if the estate lacks other funds to cover the mortgage arrears.
- Process: List the property for sale as quickly as possible. Given the urgency, setting a competitive price that ensures a quick sale while still covering the mortgage and any legal fees is essential.
- Consideration: You may need to negotiate with the mortgage lender for a short sale if the property value does not cover the mortgage balance. This involves the lender agreeing to accept less than the amount owed as full payment.

2. Refinance the Real Estate

- Refinancing: If the estate has a good credit standing and the property has substantial equity, refinancing the mortgage might be possible. Refinancing could lower the monthly payments or consolidate the arrears with a new loan.
- Eligibility: You'll need to check with lenders about refinancing options in the name of the estate. This often requires showing sufficient estate assets or income to qualify for a new loan.
- Advantage: This allows the estate to retain the property, potentially until the market conditions improve for a sale or until the estate is in a better position to decide on the property's disposition.

3. Pay Off the Back-Payments

- Catch-Up Payments: If the estate has available funds, another option is to pay off the overdue mortgage payments to bring the mortgage current and stop the foreclosure process.
- Limitations: Note that if the mortgage is a reverse mortgage, this option may not be viable as reverse mortgages require repayment upon the borrower's death or when the home is no longer the principal residence.
- Funds Utilization: Utilizing the estate's liquid assets (such as cash in bank accounts) could resolve the foreclosure without additional borrowing or selling the property.

Additional Considerations

- Legal and Financial Advice: It's advisable to consult with a real estate attorney or a financial advisor who understands foreclosure processes. They can provide guidance tailored to the specific circumstances of the estate.
- Communication with the Lender: Proactively communicating with the lender about the decedent's passing and your role as the personal representative can sometimes facilitate negotiations for refinancing or restructuring the loan.
- Impact on the Estate: Consider how each option affects the estate's overall financial health and the beneficiaries' interests. For example, refinancing might preserve the estate's assets in the short term but could lead to more significant financial obligations over time.

If you're facing foreclosure on a property within the estate, these options can provide pathways to resolve the issue, but each requires careful consideration of the estate's financial situation and the housing market dynamics. Always consider seeking professional advice to choose the best course of action. If you need assistance in evaluating these options or managing the process, please do not hesitate to contact our office.

Managing Potential Foreclosure of the Decedent's House

As the personal representative of the estate, it is critical to actively manage and monitor any potential foreclosure issues with the decedent's property. Here's a detailed guide on your responsibilities and the steps you need to take to keep the estate informed and address foreclosure risks:

1. Forward and Monitor the Decedent's Mail

- Action: Forward all mail from the decedent's address to your own to ensure you receive all correspondence, including any notices from mortgage lenders or foreclosure proceedings.

- Purpose: This allows you to stay informed about any mortgage payments that are due, overdue, or any legal notices regarding the status of the property.

2. Identify Foreclosure Risks

- Responsibility: It's crucial to determine if the house is under threat of foreclosure. Regularly checking the decedent's mail for any mortgage-related notices is key.
- Notice of Default or Trustee Sale: Look out for any formal notices such as a Notice of Default or a Notice of Trustee Sale, which are clear indications that foreclosure proceedings have begun.

3. Communicate with the Foreclosure Trustee

- Stay Informed: Establish and maintain communication with the foreclosure trustee (the entity managing the foreclosure process). This is essential to obtain up-to-date information on the foreclosure status.
- Foreclosure Sale Date: Inquire about when the foreclosure sale is set and monitor any changes or postponements to this date.

4. Notify the Estate's Attorney

- Immediate Notification: Inform your attorney immediately upon receiving any notices related to foreclosure or learning of a set date for a foreclosure sale.
- Legal Consultation: Discuss potential legal actions or interventions that might be necessary to protect the estate's interest in the property.

Legal Options to Address Foreclosure

1. TEMPORARY RESTRAINING ORDER (TRO)

- Purpose: A TRO can temporarily halt the foreclosure process, buying time to either sell, refinance the property, or catch up on overdue mortgage payments.
- Timing: A TRO must be filed within a critical timeframe, typically no later than three weeks before the scheduled foreclosure sale.
- Costs and Requirements: Filing for a TRO incurs legal costs and extraordinary attorney's fees. You'll need to provide all heirs' contact information for ex parte notice, which is required to inform interested parties about the legal action being taken.

2. PERMANENT SOLUTIONS

- Sell the Property: If the estate is unable to maintain the property or catch up on payments, selling the property might be the best option to prevent foreclosure and satisfy debts.
- Refinance: If feasible, refinancing the mortgage might allow for more manageable payment terms and prevent the loss of the property.
- Pay Off Back Payments: If the estate has sufficient funds, paying the overdue amounts to bring the mortgage current is a direct way to stop the foreclosure process. Note that this option is not available with reverse mortgages.

KEY CONSIDERATIONS

- Proactive Management: It is vital to be proactive in managing and monitoring the property's financial obligations, especially if the property is a significant asset of the estate.
- Legal Guidance: Always seek timely legal advice to navigate foreclosure risks effectively. Understanding your legal options

and the implications of each step can significantly impact the estate's best interests.

By closely monitoring the property's financial standing and promptly addressing any issues, you can better manage the estate and protect its assets. If you have any questions or need further assistance, do not hesitate to contact the legal team handling the estate.

Obtaining a Temporary Restraining Order to Delay Foreclosure

If the decedent's house is facing imminent foreclosure, one legal tool available to temporarily halt the process is a Temporary Restraining Order (TRO). This option can provide critical time to arrange a more permanent solution, such as selling the property, refinancing the mortgage, or catching up on overdue payments. Here's how the process for obtaining a TRO typically works:

WHAT IS A TEMPORARY RESTRAINING ORDER?

A TRO is a court order that temporarily halts the foreclosure process. It is not a permanent solution but can provide necessary time to arrange financial affairs or negotiate with the lender.

STEPS TO OBTAIN A TRO

1. Filing the Petition:

- Timing: A TRO can be filed close to the date of the scheduled foreclosure sale, usually within three weeks before the sale date.
- Legal Representation: Due to the complexity and urgency of filing for a TRO, it's advisable to work with an attorney who specializes in real estate or foreclosure law.

2. Requirements:

- Heir Notification: You must provide ex parte notice to all heirs of the estate. This involves informing every heir of the actions being taken, usually at short notice. Having accurate contact information for all heirs, including phone numbers, is crucial.
- Court Hearing: The request for a TRO will result in a court hearing where you must present a compelling reason for the court to halt the foreclosure temporarily. The initial TRO, if granted, typically lasts for three weeks.

3. Costs and Legal Fees:

- Attorney's Fees: Filing for a TRO involves extraordinary attorney's fees because of the urgent and specialized nature of the service.
- Court Costs: There may also be court fees associated with filing the necessary paperwork.

After Obtaining a TRO

- Permanent Solutions: During the period that the TRO is in effect, you must work towards a permanent solution to prevent the foreclosure. This could include:
- Selling the Property: If there is sufficient equity in the property, selling it may be the best option to pay off the mortgage.
- Refinancing: If the estate or heirs can qualify for refinancing, this could reduce the mortgage payments or consolidate overdue payments into a new loan.
- Paying Off Back Payments: If possible, use estate funds or arrange for contributions from heirs to catch up on back payments to cure the default.

Considerations

- Impact on Credit and Legal Standing: It's important to note that stopping a foreclosure via a TRO does not resolve the

underlying financial issue and can impact the estate's or heirs' credit and legal standing.
- Negotiations with Lender: Often, a more feasible solution can be reached by negotiating directly with the lender for a loan modification, repayment plan, or other settlement arrangements.

Conclusion

While a TRO can provide a temporary reprieve from foreclosure, it is crucial to have a strategy for addressing the mortgage default more permanently. The costs and effort involved in obtaining a TRO should be weighed against other options available to the estate. If you need assistance or have questions about pursuing a TRO or exploring other options to handle the foreclosure, please contact our office. We can guide you through the process or refer you to a qualified attorney to handle the specifics of the foreclosure defense.

Consequences of Not Properly Handling Foreclosure of the Decedent's House

When managing an estate, it is crucial to address any pending foreclosure on the decedent's house promptly. Failing to do so can lead to significant consequences that may adversely affect the estate and the beneficiaries. Here's what you need to know:

Loss of Property

- Trustee Sale: If the foreclosure process concludes without intervention, the house may be sold at a trustee sale. Once the property is sold at this auction, the estate loses any claim to the property.
- Irreversibility: After a trustee sale, there is no opportunity to reclaim the property. This is a final action, and the property will then belong to the highest bidder at the sale.

Financial Implications

- Deficiency: In the event the sale price at auction does not cover the mortgage balance and associated costs (which is common), the property is sold, but the deficiency remains. However, in many states, lenders may not seek deficiency judgments on certain types of loans, such as non-recourse loans or primary residential properties, depending on state law.
- Surplus Funds: On rare occasions, if the property sells for more than the debt owed, there may be surplus funds. However, these instances are uncommon because properties in foreclosure often sell for less than their market value.

Legal and Administrative Complications

- Distribution of Surplus: If there are surplus funds from the sale, the mortgage company might face difficulties in determining who is entitled to these funds, especially since the borrower has deceased. This can lead to the funds being interpleaded—deposited with the court until it can determine the rightful recipient(s).
- Probate Proceedings: Even if surplus funds exist, accessing these funds generally requires going through probate proceedings to legally establish entitlement under the supervision of the court.

Steps to Avoid Negative Outcomes

- Proactive Management: To avoid these consequences, it's vital to manage the foreclosure proactively:
- Communication with Lender: Immediately inform the lender of the borrower's death and your role as personal representative. Negotiate with the lender for a possible modification, forbearance, or other arrangement to delay or prevent foreclosure.
- Legal Actions: Consider legal actions such as applying for a

temporary restraining order to delay the sale, allowing more time to refinance or sell the property on more favorable terms.
- Sell or Refinance: If the estate has equity in the property and it is financially feasible, selling the property before foreclosure or refinancing to pay off the existing mortgage can preserve the estate's assets and potentially provide a better financial return to the beneficiaries.

Conclusion

The key to managing a decedent's property under threat of foreclosure is early and effective intervention. Ignoring foreclosure notices or failing to act promptly can lead to irreversible financial and legal consequences that complicate the estate's administration and potentially diminish the value passed on to heirs. If the estate is facing such issues, it's advisable to consult with a real estate or foreclosure attorney to explore all available options to protect the estate's interests.

Managing Cash and Bank Accounts in the Decedent's Estate

As the personal representative, part of your responsibility involves handling the decedent's cash and bank accounts effectively and lawfully. Here's a guide on how to deal with these assets:

Cash

What We Need from You:

- Reporting Cash on Hand: Inform us of the exact amount of cash the decedent had on hand at the time of their death. This includes any cash found in the decedent's residence, in safety deposit boxes, or any other locations where the decedent might have kept cash.

Action Required:

- Depositing Cash: All cash that was in the decedent's possession at the time of death should be carefully counted and deposited into a new bank account that you will open in the name of the estate. This account will be used to manage all estate transactions moving forward.

Checks

What We Need from You:

- Photocopies of Checks: Please provide photocopies of any checks you find that were made payable to the decedent or to the estate of the decedent. This includes checks that may not have been deposited prior to the decedent's passing.

Action Required:

- Depositing Checks: All checks made payable to the decedent or the estate should be deposited into the estate's bank account. This ensures that these funds are properly accounted for and managed according to probate laws.

Opening an Estate Bank Account

1. Documentation Needed: To open a bank account for the estate, you will generally need the decedent's death certificate, a copy of the will (if applicable), and the Letters of Administration or Letters Testamentary that grant you the authority to act on behalf of the estate.
2. Choosing a Bank: You can choose any bank, but it may be simplest to use the bank where the decedent held their accounts, as they may already have certain information and can facilitate the transfer of funds.
3. Purpose of the Account: The estate bank account will be used to gather all liquid assets of the estate, pay any debts, ongoing

expenses, and eventually distribute the remaining funds to the heirs as dictated by the will or state law.

Using Estate Funds

- Paying Debates and Expenses: Estate funds should be used to pay any debts, taxes, and administrative expenses associated with the estate. Keep detailed records of all transactions to ensure transparency and accountability.
- Distribution to Heirs: Only after all debts and expenses have been settled, and upon approval by the probate court, should the remaining funds be distributed to the heirs.

Record-Keeping

- Maintain Records: It's crucial to maintain meticulous records of all financial transactions involving the estate's funds. This includes deposits, withdrawals, payments, and distributions. These records are important for both accounting purposes and for providing required reports to the probate court.

Handling cash and bank accounts in an estate requires careful attention to detail and adherence to legal guidelines. By following these steps, you ensure that the estate's financial assets are managed properly, paving the way for a smooth administration process. If you have any questions or need further assistance with any of these steps, please feel free to contact our office.

Handling Bank Accounts in the Decedent's Estate

As the personal representative of the estate, one of your responsibilities is to manage the decedent's bank accounts effectively. This includes ensuring that all funds within these accounts are properly accounted for from the date of the decedent's death until these accounts are closed. Here is what you need to do and what I need from you to manage this process:

What We Need from You

1. Bank Statements:

- From Date of Death: You will need to gather bank statements starting from the statement period that includes the date of death.
- Until Account Closure: Continue collecting statements until each account is officially closed. This ensures that all transactions are accounted for during the probate process.
- All Pages Required: It's important to include all pages of each bank statement, not just the pages that contain transaction lists. If a bank statement says: "Page 1 of 4," all four pages are needed, even if some pages include only advertisements or seemingly irrelevant information.

Steps to Follow

1. ACCESS AND NOTIFY THE BANK:

- Death Notification: Notify each bank where the decedent held an account about their death. Provide a copy of the death certificate and your Letters of Administration or Letters Testamentary. This notification will usually freeze the accounts to prevent unauthorized transactions.

2. COLLECT DOCUMENTATION:

- Gather Statements: As mentioned, collect all bank statements from the period including and following the date of death. If you don't have access to the decedent's online banking, you may need to request these statements directly from the bank.
- Statement Details: Ensure that you review each statement for any automatic deposits or withdrawals that need to be addressed, such as stopping automatic bill payments or notifying recipients of direct deposits that the account holder has deceased.

3. *Open an Estate Bank Account:*

- New Account for Estate: Open a new bank account in the name of the estate. This account will be used to consolidate the liquid assets of the estate and manage all incoming and outgoing payments, such as paying off debts and eventually distributing money to heirs.

4. *Transfer Funds:*

- From Decedent's Accounts: Once all matters such as debts and recurring payments are settled, transfer the remaining funds from the decedent's accounts into the estate's bank account.

5. *Close Decedent's Accounts:*

- Final Closure: After transferring funds and ensuring all pending transactions are cleared, formally close the decedent's bank accounts. Obtain documentation from the bank confirming the closure of these accounts.

Stage 3C: The Decedent's Bank Account ™

Step	Tasks to Complete	What WE do	What YOU do	Estimated Time Frame
3C1	Go to the Decedent's Bank	We provide you with a letter to take to the Decedent's bank	You bring to a bank: 1. Letters 2. Order for Probate 3. Death Certificate 4. IRS EIN letter Your I.D.	As soon as the Court issues Letters to You
3C2	Required Bank Statements		You get the bank statements from the date of death through the date that you withdraw all funds	As soon as the Court issues Letters to You
3C3	Decedent's Funds		You obtain a check for the remaining balance of the bank accounts	As soon as the Court issues Letters to You
3C4	Close the Decedent's Bank Accounts		You close the Decedent's bank accounts	As soon as the Court issues Letters to You

© 2024 ProbateDocs LLC

Stage 3C: Open an Estate Bank Account ™

Step	Tasks to Complete	What WE do	What YOU do	Estimated Time Frame
3C1	Estate Bank Account Requirements	The estate bank account must be: 1. At a California branch 2. Earn interest 3. Be FDIC insured	You choose which bank to open the estate bank account	As soon as the Court issues Letters to You
3C2	If You Are In California		You bring to a bank: 5. Letters 6. Order for Probate 7. Death Certificate 8. IRS EIN letter 9. Your I.D.	As soon as the Court issues Letters to You
3C3	If You Live Outside California and Cannot Be Here	We refer a bank that will allow you to sign the estate bank documents from outside of California	You follow the instructions from the bank to sign the documents to open the estate bank account	Approximately 15 – 30 days to open the account
3C4	Deposit Funds in the Estate Bank Account		You deposit the estate's funds in the estate bank account	Anytime you receive estate funds
3C5	Pay Bills From the Estate Bank Account		You can pay the administrative expenses and creditor claims, but not yourself	Anytime, so long as the estate is solvent
3C6	Bank Statements		You give Us copies of all bank statements	From the month you open the account forward
3C6	Do Not Give Funds to Heirs Until the Court Orders Distribution		You cannot pay yourself or distribute any funds to an heir without a court order	Only after the judge signs the Order for Distribution

© 2024 ProbateDocs LLC

Important Considerations

- Record-Keeping: Keep meticulous records of all transactions involving the decedent's bank accounts, including dates, amounts, and purposes of all transfers. This will be crucial for estate accounting and reporting to the court.
- Communication with Financial Institutions: Maintain clear and consistent communication with the banks holding the

decedent's accounts. This helps ensure that all actions taken are documented and authorized.
- Legal Compliance: Ensure compliance with all legal requirements and court orders regarding the management of the decedent's assets.

By following these steps and requirements, you help ensure that the estate's financial affairs are handled accurately and legally. If you have any questions or need assistance with any of these processes, do not hesitate to contact our office. We are here to support you through each step of managing the estate.

Appraising the Decedent's Tangible Personal Property

Appraising tangible personal property is a crucial part of estate administration. It involves assessing the value of personal items belonging to the decedent at the time of their death. This information is important for accurately documenting the estate's assets for both probate purposes and fair distribution to heirs. Here's how you can help in gathering the necessary information for this appraisal process:

Information Required for Appraisal

1. LIST OF PERSONAL PROPERTY:

- General Categories: Group common items into categories for easier documentation and appraisal. Common categories include:
- Household Furniture and Furnishings: Sofas, beds, tables, etc.
- Clothing and Costume Jewelry: Everyday wear, suits, dresses, and non-valuable jewelry.
- Tools and Equipment: Hand tools, power tools, garden tools, etc.

2. *HIGH-VALUE ITEMS LISTED SEPARATELY:*

- Specific Identification Needed: Any personal property item that might have significant value should be listed separately with detailed descriptions. For example:
- Men's Rolex Oyster Perpetual Wristwatch: Note the type of metal, any unique features, and condition.
- Lady's Gold Ring with Two Large White Stones: Describe the stones (e.g., diamonds, cubic zirconia) and any markings.
- 1861 "S" $20.00 Gold Piece (U.S.) in Uncirculated Condition: Specify the coin's condition, year, and any special attributes.
- Original Oil Painting "Sierra Lake" by Elmer Wachetel (1925): Include the artist's name, title of the work, and the year if known.
- Glock Handgun Model 21, Serial Number 26549: List the make, model, and serial number.

Stage 3D: Tangible Personal Property ™

Step	Tasks to Complete	What WE do	What YOU do	Estimated Time Frame
3D1	Notify Heirs of Disposition of Tangible Personal Property	We draft and mail a Notice to heirs of how you will dispose of Tangible Personal Property	You inform Us of what You will do with the Tangible Personal Property	After the Court issues Letters to You
3D2	Option 1: Distribute to Heirs	We draft a receipt for You to have heirs sign for what they receive (We pay the eFiling fee from Your deposit)	You have a fair way for heirs to receive what they want, have them sign a receipt for what they receive	Time varies, with complexity of Your case and when You can coordinate with the heirs
3D3	Option 2: Sell What You Can		You sell what the heirs do not want, or hire an Estate Agent to sell for You	Time varies, with complexity of Your case and when You can sell the Tangible Personal Property
3D4	Option 3: Donate What Does Not Sell		You donate to charity what does not sell	Time varies, with complexity of Your case and when You can donate the Tangible Personal Property
3D5	Option 4: Throw Away the Rest		You throw away what you cannot donate to charity	Time varies, with complexity of Your case and when You can throw out the Tangible Personal Property

© 2024 ProbateDocs LLC

Process for Appraisal

1. DOCUMENTING AND PHOTOGRAPHING ITEMS:

- Detailed Records: Create a detailed list and take photographs of each item, especially those of higher value. This visual documentation can be very helpful for the appraiser.
- Condition Notes: Note the condition of each item, as this greatly affects the value. Conditions might range from poor to excellent.

2. Professional Appraisal:

- Engage an Appraiser: For high-value items or collections (e.g., art, jewelry, antiques), it might be necessary to engage a professional appraiser who specializes in those types of items.
- Appraisal Event: The appraiser will review the items and provide estimates based on current market values, considering the condition, rarity, and provenance of each item.

3. Compile Inventory for Probate:

- Inventory Submission: Combine the general categories and specific high-value items into a comprehensive inventory list.
- Valuation Report: The appraiser's valuation report should be attached to the inventory when submitted to the probate court.

Legal and Practical Considerations

- Fair Market Value: Appraisals should reflect the fair market value of items as of the date of the decedent's death.
- Use of Appraisals: These valuations are used for determining estate taxes, dividing assets among heirs, or potentially for sale.
- Ethical Handling: Ensure that all items are appraised and reported honestly to avoid potential disputes among beneficiaries or with tax authorities.

By providing a detailed and organized list of the decedent's tangible personal property, you facilitate a smoother appraisal process. This thorough documentation helps ensure that all assets are accounted for and valued appropriately, supporting transparent and equitable estate administration. If you have any questions about specific items or need assistance in arranging for professional appraisals, please reach out to our office.

Understanding Specialty Appraisals in Estate Administration

When managing an estate, it's crucial to accurately value all assets for both equitable distribution and tax purposes. While a probate referee can handle the appraisal of general personal property items, high-value or specialty items often require specialized appraisal expertise. Here's an overview of when and why specialty appraisals are necessary and how to go about obtaining them.

WHAT CONSTITUTES SPECIALTY APPRAISALS?

Specialty appraisals are used for items that require specific expertise to determine their market value due to their unique characteristics, such as rarity, age, or technical aspects. These items typically include:

- Jewelry: High-value pieces like diamond rings, antique jewelry, or items with precious stones and metals.
- Art: Original paintings, sculptures, limited edition prints, and other valuable artworks.
- Antiques and Collectibles: Items with historical significance or those that are rare and old, such as vintage furniture, coins, stamps, and other collectibles.
- Exotic or Classic Cars: Vehicles that may have significant value due to their make, model, vintage status, or rarity.
- Specialty Electronics or Musical Instruments: High-end audio equipment, vintage instruments, or rare technological items.

WHY SPECIALTY APPRAISALS ARE NEEDED

1. Accuracy: Specialty appraisers have the expertise to assess the true market value of complex items, considering factors like condition, provenance, and current market trends.
2. Legal and Tax Compliance: Accurate appraisals ensure that the estate complies with tax regulations and helps prevent future legal challenges regarding asset distribution.

3. Insurance: Proper valuation is also essential for insuring high-value items within the estate.

How to Obtain Specialty Appraisals

1. Identify the Need: Review the estate's inventory to identify items that require specialty appraisals. This might be evident from the decedent's insurance policies, purchase records, or family knowledge.
2. Select Qualified Appraisers: Choose appraisers who specialize in the relevant type of item. For instance:

- Jewelry: Go to a certified gemologist at a reputable jewelry store or an independent appraiser who specializes in fine jewelry.
- Art: Contact an art appraiser who is knowledgeable about the specific type of art or the artist.
- Antiques: Look for an appraiser with expertise in the specific era or type of antique.

3. Document the Appraisal: Ensure that the appraiser provides a detailed report that includes descriptions, the basis of the valuation, and the appraiser's qualifications and signatures.
4. Coordinate with the Probate Referee: Inform the probate referee of the specialty appraisals, as these will complement the general appraisal of the estate's assets.

Practical Steps

- Schedule Appointments: Make appointments with the selected appraisers and ensure that they can access the items to be appraised.
- Prepare Documentation: Gather any documentation related to the items, such as receipts, previous appraisals, or certificates of authenticity, which can assist the appraiser.
- Review Appraisals: Once completed, review the appraisal reports for accuracy and completeness. Confirm that they

meet the necessary legal standards for inclusion in the estate's inventory.

Specialty appraisals are a critical component of estate management, particularly when dealing with high-value or unique items. These appraisals not only ensure compliance with legal standards but also help in accurately determining the estate's total value for equitable distribution to beneficiaries. If you need assistance identifying suitable appraisers or managing this process, please contact our office.

Managing the Decedent's Tangible Personal Property

As the personal representative, you have specific responsibilities and options regarding the handling of the decedent's tangible personal property. Here's a structured guide on how to manage these items according to the estate's requirements and California law:

Restrictions and General Guidelines

1. Location Restrictions:

- The personal property of the decedent must not be removed from California until it is legally distributed.

2. Distribution Timing:

- Personal property should only be distributed to the heirs during the final distribution phase of the probate process, not before.

Options for Disposing of Personal Property

1. *Distribution to Heirs:*

- Preferred Items: If certain heirs desire specific items, and it aligns with the will (if present) or agreed upon equitably among the heirs, these items can be earmarked for distribution accordingly.
- Written Notice: We must provide a written notice to all heirs detailing the items to be distributed, ensuring transparency.

2. *Sale:*

- Estate Sale or Garage Sale: Selling the personal property through an estate sale or garage sale is a viable option to convert assets into cash that can be distributed or used for settling debts.
- Preparation for Sale: Inventory all items to be sold and ensure they are appropriately appraised or valued.

3. *Donation:*

- Charitable Giving: Items that are not wanted by heirs or are not feasible to sell can be donated to charity.
- Documentation: Obtain receipts for donated items, as this can be beneficial for tax purposes and estate records.

4. *Abandonment:*

- Cost Considerations: If certain properties cost more to store or collect than their value, they may be officially abandoned.
- Legal Process: Ensure that the abandonment process adheres to local regulations to avoid future liabilities.

5. DISPOSAL:

- Unwanted or Broken Items: Dispose of any items that are broken, outdated, or otherwise considered junk.
- Eco-friendly Disposal: Consider environmentally responsible disposal methods to handle electronic and hazardous waste properly.

Steps Before Disposal

1. INVENTORY AND NOTIFICATION:

- List Creation: Before disposing of any personal property, create a detailed list of all items and their proposed handling (sold, donated, abandoned, thrown away).
- Approval: Submit this list to our office. We will prepare the necessary notice for you to sign, ensuring all legal requirements are met and heirs are duly informed.

2. RECORD KEEPING:

- Documentation: Keep thorough records of how each item is handled, including sales receipts, donation receipts, and notes on items disposed of or abandoned.
- Transparency: This documentation will be crucial for final estate accounting and might be required by the probate court.

Final Distribution

- Remaining Items: Any items not sold, donated, abandoned, or thrown away should be held for distribution among the heirs as per the final instructions of the probate process.

Conclusion

Handling the tangible personal property of a decedent requires careful consideration of legal guidelines, heir expectations, and the value and condition of the items involved. By following the outlined procedures, you can ensure that the property is managed responsibly, maximizing the value returned to the estate and its beneficiaries. If you have any questions or need assistance with this process, please do not hesitate to contact our office.

Appraising the Decedent's Vehicle

To accurately appraise the decedent's vehicle as part of the estate inventory and appraisal process, specific information about each vehicle is required. Here's a detailed list of the information needed and why each item is important:

Information Required for Vehicle Appraisal

1. YEAR, MAKE, AND MODEL

- Details: Specify the year of manufacture, the make (brand), and the model of the vehicle. This basic information is crucial as it forms the foundation of the vehicle's valuation.

2. APPROXIMATE MILEAGE AS OF THE DATE OF DEATH

- Importance: The mileage on the vehicle significantly affects its value. Lower mileage typically indicates less wear and tear and therefore a higher value.

3. Vehicle Identification Number (VIN)

- Verification: A VIN is essential for confirming the vehicle's identity and for checking against databases for any liens, accident history, or recalls.
- How to Provide:
- Registration: This document will have the VIN and proof of the owner.
- Title Document: Shows ownership and VIN.
- Picture of the VIN: A clear photo of the VIN plate usually found on the dashboard or driver's side door frame.

4. Condition of the Vehicle

- Categories: You will need to assess the condition of the vehicle, which helps in determining its value. Categories typically include:
- Excellent: The vehicle looks new, has excellent mechanical condition, and shows minimal to no wear.
- Good: Free from major defects, may have minor body blemishes or interior wear, no major mechanical problems.
- Fair: Has some mechanical or cosmetic defects, needs servicing but is in reasonable running condition.
- Poor: Has severe mechanical or cosmetic defects and is in poor running condition.
- Inoperable: The vehicle does not run and may require significant investment to be functional.

Stage 3E: Vehicles ™

Step	Tasks to Complete	What WE do	What YOU do	Estimated Time Frame
3E1	Do Not Drive the Vehicle	Driving the vehicle reduces its value and adds liability to the Estate	You keep insurance on the vehicle and safeguard it	Beginning from the date of death until you transfer the vehicle
3E2	Information We Need		Give Us the year, make, model, mileage, title with VIN, and condition	
3E3	Option 1: Distribute to an Heir	We draft a Notice of Proposed Action to distribute the vehicle to an heir for its Appraised value, starts a 15-day deadline for anyone to object (We pay the eFiling fee from Your deposit)	You confirm that the estate is solvent and everyone consents for the distribution and transfer the vehicle with the DMV or AAA	Time varies, with complexity of Your case and when You can distribute the vehicle to the heir
3E4	Option 2: Sell the Vehicle to an Heir	We draft a Notice of Proposed Action to sell the vehicle to an heir, starts a 15-day deadline for anyone to object (We pay the eFiling fee from Your deposit)	You sell the vehicle to an heir through the DMV or AAA	Time varies, with complexity of Your case and when You can sell the vehicle
3E5	Option 3: Return the Vehicle to the Finance Company		You return the vehicle to the finance company - Leased vehicles or vehicles that have a loan are not owed by the Decedent	Time varies, with complexity of Your case and when You can return the vehicle
3E6	Option 4: Sell the Vehicle to a Third Party		You sell the vehicle to a third party or car dealership	Time varies, with complexity of Your case and when You sell the vehicle

© 2024 ProbateDocs LLC

Process for Appraisal

- Gathering Information: Collect all the above details for each vehicle. This includes inspecting the vehicle, locating documents, and possibly consulting with a mechanic to verify the mechanical condition if uncertain.
- Appraisal: Once all information is gathered, an appraiser or a valuation service can use this data to estimate the fair market value of the vehicle. For estate purposes, it's beneficial to use a professional appraiser or a recognized pricing guide like Kelley Blue Book or NADA Guides.
- Documentation: Keep a record of all findings and the final

appraisal report. This documentation will be part of the estate's inventory filed with the probate court.

Why Accurate Appraisal is Important

- Estate Valuation: Accurate appraisal impacts the overall valuation of the estate, affecting estate taxes, division among heirs, or sale decisions.
- Legal Compliance: Provides a defensible valuation in case of disputes or audits by tax authorities.

Conclusion

The careful documentation and appraisal of the decedent's vehicles are crucial for effective estate management. If you need assistance in evaluating the condition of the vehicles or in arranging for professional appraisal services, please do not hesitate to contact our office. We are here to ensure that every aspect of the estate administration is handled competently and compliantly.

Information Required for the Decedent's Mobile Home

When handling the estate of the decedent, it is important to accurately appraise all assets, including mobile homes. To ensure a thorough and accurate appraisal of the decedent's mobile home, specific details are needed. Here's what you should provide to facilitate this process:

Essential Information for Mobile Home Appraisal

1. *YEAR, MAKE, & MODEL:*

- Details: Identify the year the mobile home was manufactured, the make (brand), and the model. This basic information is crucial for determining the baseline value.

2. *SIZE:*

- Dimensions: Provide the dimensions of the mobile home, typically in feet (e.g., 24 ft. x 58 ft.). This helps in assessing the living space and, consequently, its market value.

3. *SERIAL NUMBER:*

- Identification: The serial number acts as the unique identifier for the mobile home and is essential for verification and registration purposes.

4. *LOCATION:*

- Address: Specify the exact location or address where the mobile home is situated. Location can significantly influence the value due to varying land values and community attributes.

5. *CONDITION AND REPAIRS:*

- Current State: Report any known issues with the mobile home or any repairs that are needed. This includes structural problems, utilities issues (plumbing, heating, electrical), or any damage to the interior or exterior.
- Impact on Value: Details about the condition are vital as they directly affect the valuation. For example, a well-maintained

home will have a higher value compared to one that requires significant repairs.

Why This Information Is Necessary

- Appraisal Accuracy: Gathering detailed and accurate information about the mobile home allows the appraiser to provide a more precise estimate of its value.
- Legal and Tax Compliance: Proper documentation and valuation of the mobile home are important for meeting probate requirements and ensuring correct tax calculations.
- Estate Planning and Distribution: Accurate valuation is crucial for fair distribution of the estate's assets among heirs or for potential sale purposes.

Stage 3E: Mobile Homes ™

Step	Tasks to Complete	What WE do	What YOU do	Estimated Time Frame
3E1	Safeguard the Mobile Home		You keep insurance on the mobile home and safeguard it	Beginning from the date of death until you transfer the mobile home
3E2	Information We Need		Give Us the year, make, model, size, serial number, and address	Time varies, with when You can give Us the information
3E3	Option 1: Distribute to an Heir	We draft a Notice of Proposed Action to distribute the mobile home to an heir for its Appraised value, starts a 15-day deadline for anyone to object (We pay the eFiling fee from Your deposit)	You confirm that the estate is solvent and everyone consents for the distribution and transfer the mobile home with the Dept. of Housing and Community Development	Time varies, with complexity of Your case and when You can distribute the mobile home to the heir
3E4	Option 2: Sell the Mobile Home to an Heir	We draft a Notice of Proposed Action to sell the mobile home to an heir, starts a 15-day deadline for anyone to object (We pay the eFiling fee from Your deposit)	You sell the mobile home to an heir through the Dept. of Housing and Community Development	Time varies, with complexity of Your case and when You can sell the mobile home
3E5	Option 4: Sell the Mobile Home to a Third Party		You sell the mobile home to a third party	Time varies, with complexity of Your case and when You sell the mobile home

© 2024 ProbateDocs LLC

Steps to Follow

- Documentation Collection: Assemble all relevant documents related to the mobile home, such as purchase documents, previous appraisal reports, and maintenance records.
- Professional Appraisal: It may be advisable to hire a professional appraiser specializing in mobile homes. They can consider all factors, including market trends and the home's condition, to provide a valid appraisal.
- Report Submission: Submit the collected information and the appraisal report to the estate's executor or attorney to be included in the estate inventory.

Conclusion

Providing comprehensive details about the decedent's mobile home is crucial for its proper valuation and handling within the estate. This information not only aids in accurate estate valuation but also ensures compliance with legal standards and helps in resolving inheritance matters efficiently. If you need assistance in gathering this information or require a professional appraisal, please do not hesitate to contact our office.

Creating an Inventory and Appraisal for the Decedent's Brokerage Accounts

As part of the estate administration process, a detailed inventory and appraisal of the decedent's brokerage accounts are essential. This information helps in accurately determining the estate's value for both probate and tax purposes. Here's what you need to provide to assist in this process:

Required Information for Each Brokerage Account

1. FINANCIAL STATEMENTS:

- Scope: You need to provide each financial statement for the brokerage accounts that includes stocks, bonds, and mutual funds, starting from the one covering the date of death.
- Duration: Continue to provide these statements up until the point you close the brokerage account.
- Complete Documents: Ensure that all pages of each financial statement are included, even if some pages contain only advertisements or seemingly irrelevant information. If a statement is marked as "Page 1 of 4," all four pages must be provided.

2. Details for Each Security Held in the Accounts:

- Number of Shares: Report the exact number of shares for each security held within the account (e.g., 350 shares).
- Type of Shares: Specify the type of shares, such as common stock, preferred stock, etc.
- Company Name: Provide the full name of the company for each security (e.g., Apple Inc.).
- Ticker Symbol and Exchange: Include the ticker symbol and the exchange on which the security is traded if applicable (e.g., NASDAQ: AAPL).
- CUSIP Number: The CUSIP number is a unique identifier for securities in the United States and Canada, which helps in precisely identifying the securities held (e.g., 037833100).

Steps to Follow

1. *Contact the Brokerage:* Reach out to the brokerage firm where the decedent had accounts. You may need to provide documentation such as a death certificate and Letters Testamentary or Letters of Administration to access or manage the accounts.
2. *Request Detailed Statements:* Request that the brokerage provide detailed statements as described above, if you do not already have access to these through online management systems or regular mailings.
3. *Record and Organize Data:* As you collect each statement and details about each security, organize this information systematically. This will be crucial for creating a comprehensive inventory and appraisal.
4. *Appraisal of Securities:* The values for stocks, bonds, and mutual funds will be based on their market values as of the date of the decedent's death. This appraisal is often handled by a probate referee or appraiser, who may need detailed information about each security to provide an accurate valuation.

Stage 3F: Stocks and Bonds ™

Step	Tasks to Complete	What WE do	What YOU do	Estimated Time Frame
3F1	Go to the Decedent's Financial Institution	We provide you with a letter to take to the Decedent's financial institution	You bring to the financial institution: 1. Letters 2. Order for Probate 3. Death Certificate 4. IRS EIN letter 5. Your I.D.	As soon as the Court issues Letters to You
3F2	Monthly Statements		You get the monthly statements from the date of death through the date that you close the brokerage account	As soon as the Court issues Letters to You
3F3	CUSIP Numbers		You ask the financial institution for the CUSIP Number for each stock, bond, or mutual fund	As soon as the Court issues Letters to You
3F4	The Estate's Brokerage Account		You open a brokerage account in your name as the personal representative of the estate (i.e., "John Doe, Executor of the Estate of Sally Doe")	As soon as the Court issues Letters to You
3F5	Close the Decedent's Brokerage Accounts		You close the Decedent's brokerage accounts	As soon as the Court issues Letters to You

© 2024 ProbateDocs LLC

Legal and Financial Considerations

- Timeliness: It's important to act promptly in gathering and providing this information to meet any deadlines imposed by the probate court or tax authorities.
- Accuracy: Ensure all provided information is accurate to prevent any legal complications or discrepancies during the probate process.

By following these guidelines and providing complete and detailed information about the decedent's brokerage accounts, you will assist in the smooth administration of the estate. If you have any questions or need assistance in obtaining any of this information, please feel free to contact our office.

Subpoena for Decedent's Brokerage Account Records

As part of managing the estate, it is crucial to obtain a comprehensive inventory and appraisal of the decedent's assets, including brokerage accounts. If you are unable to gather the necessary financial statements for the decedent's brokerage accounts, we have the option to subpoena these records. Here's how the process works and what it involves:

Importance of Timely Information Collection

- Court Deadlines: The probate court requires that an inventory and appraisal of the estate's assets be filed within four months of the issuance of the Letters of Administration or Letters Testamentary.
- Initial Request: We ask that you attempt to obtain the financial statements within 15 days of being tasked with this responsibility. This allows us to meet court deadlines and manage the estate efficiently.

Subpoena Process

- Initiation: If the necessary documents are not obtained within 15 days, our policy is to proceed with a subpoena to secure these records from the financial institutions or brokerage firms.
- Duration: The process of issuing a subpoena and obtaining the records can take approximately 45 days. This includes the time to prepare the subpoena, serve it to the institution, and allow them time to comply.

Costs and Fees

- Extraordinary Fees and Costs: Subpoenaing records involves additional legal work, which incurs extraordinary fees and costs. These are over and above the typical estate administration expenses.

- Budget Impact: These costs will be charged to the estate, and it is important to consider this in the estate's budget planning.

Legal Considerations

- Legal Authority: As the personal representative, you have the legal authority to request these documents and, if necessary, subpoena them under the court's oversight.
- Compliance by Institutions: Financial institutions are legally obligated to comply with subpoenas and provide the requested documents, ensuring that we can complete the inventory and appraisal accurately.

Steps Following Subpoena

- Review and Appraisal: Once the records are obtained, they will be reviewed to determine the value of each asset as of the date of death. This information is critical for the accurate appraisal of the estate.
- Filing with the Court: The completed inventory and appraisal will be filed with the court, adhering to the stipulated timelines to ensure the smooth progression of the probate process.

Communication

- Ongoing Updates: We will keep you informed throughout the process, from the issuance of the subpoena to the receipt and analysis of the financial records.
- Support: Should you have any questions or require assistance at any stage, please do not hesitate to contact our office.

It's important to manage this process efficiently to avoid delays and additional costs. If securing these financial records proves challenging, we are prepared to take the necessary legal steps to ensure compliance and meet our probate deadlines.

Giving Notice to Creditors in the Probate Process

As part of managing the decedent's estate, it is crucial to address any outstanding debts properly. The process involves identifying creditors, notifying them of the decedent's passing, and providing them with an opportunity to file claims for any amounts owed. Here's what you need to do to help manage this responsibility:

Steps to Identify and Notify Creditors

1. *Review Decedent's Mail:*

- Action Required: Open and read through the decedent's mail to identify any ongoing financial obligations. Look for bills, loan statements, credit card statements, medical bills, utility bills, and other similar documents.
- Importance: This helps in compiling a comprehensive list of potential creditors who may have valid claims against the estate.

2. *Provide Copies of Bills or Invoices:*

- Documentation: Forward copies of any bills, invoices, or statements that indicate an outstanding debt owed by the decedent.
- Details to Include: Ensure that each document includes the creditor's contact information, the amount owed, and any account numbers or reference numbers.

3. *Legal Implications of Non-Notification:*

- Personal Liability: If you fail to give notice to a creditor that you knew or reasonably should have known about, you could be held personally liable for that debt. This underscores the importance of thorough review and reporting.

4. *Notice to Creditors:*

- Procedure: We will prepare and send out a Notice to Creditors to all identified creditors based on the information you provide. This formal notice informs creditors of their right to file a claim against the estate.
- Deadline for Claims: Creditors are typically given a set period by law (often four months from the date of the notice) to file their claims with the probate court.

5. *Creditor's Responsibility:*

- Filing a Claim: It is up to each creditor to file a formal creditor claim with the court within the allowed timeframe.
- Verification: The estate has the right to dispute any claims that are incorrect or fraudulent.

6. *Special Consideration for Funeral Expenses:*

- Funeral Costs: Whoever paid the funeral expenses is considered a creditor of the estate and must file a creditor claim to be reimbursed from the estate's assets.
- Documentation: Ensure that a detailed invoice or receipt for funeral expenses is available to support the claim.

Stage 3G: Creditor Notices ™

Step	Tasks to Complete	What WE do	What YOU do	Estimated Time Frame
3G1	Notify Creditors	We draft and mail a Notice to Creditors (We pay the eFiling fee from Your deposit)	You inform Us of any creditors that you know, or reasonably should have known	Within two months of the Court issuing Letters to You
3G2	Notify Medi-Cal	We draft and mail a notice to the Department of Health Care Services for Medi-Cal for the Decedent and pre-deceased spouse, if needed (We pay the eFiling fee from Your deposit)	You inform Us if the Decedent had a pre-deceased spouse who received Medi-Cal benefits	After the Court issues Letters to You
3G3	Notify Franchise Tax Board	We draft and mail a notice to the Franchise Tax Board for taxes (We pay the eFiling fee from Your deposit)		After the Court issues Letters to You
3G4	Notify Victims Compensation Board	We draft and mail a notice to the Victims Compensation Board for restitution (We pay the eFiling fee from Your deposit)	You inform Us if any heir has been previously incarcerated in California	Within two months of the Court issuing Letters to You
3G5	Notify Other State Agencies	We draft and mail a notice to other California agencies, as needed (We pay the eFiling fee from Your deposit)	You inform Us of any other California agencies that may need notice	Within two months of the Court issuing Letters to You

© 2024 ProbateDocs LLC

Stage 3G: Creditor Claims ™

Step	Tasks to Complete	What WE do	What YOU do	Estimated Time Frame
3G1	Creditor Claim	We send the Creditor Claim to You	You choose whether to accept or reject the creditor claim	As soon as We receive a creditor claim
3G2	Acceptance or Rejection	We draft an Acceptance or Rejection of Creditor Claim, based on your choice	You sign the Acceptance or Rejection of Creditor Claim, based on your choice	Within three business days of Your choice to accept or reject
3G3	Mail and File the Acceptance or Rejection	We mail the Acceptance or Rejection to the creditor and file with the Court – We pay the eFile fee with your retainer deposit		Within three business days of You signing the Acceptance or Rejection
3G4	Creditor Sues on the Rejected Claim	We notify you if the creditor has sued the estate		Creditor has 90 days to sue the Estate on the rejected Creditor Claim
3G5	You Pay the Accepted Claim from the Estate Funds		You pay the accepted Creditor Claim from the Estate's funds, so long as the Estate is solvent	Anytime, so long as the estate is solvent
3G6	Satisfaction of Accepted Claim	We file the Satisfaction of Claim with the Court (We pay the eFiling fee from Your deposit)	You request a Satisfaction of Claim from the creditor	Within three business days of receiving the Satisfaction of Claim

© 2024 ProbateDocs LLC

Why Accurate Handling of Creditors is Important

- Avoiding Legal Complications: Proper notification and handling of creditor claims help prevent legal challenges against the estate, which can delay the probate process and potentially diminish the estate's value due to prolonged legal fees and disputes.
- Fair Distribution: Ensuring all debts are identified and settled allows for a fair and equitable distribution of the remaining estate assets to the heirs.

Conclusion

Carefully managing the identification and notification of creditors is a critical responsibility in estate administration. By systematically reviewing the decedent's mail and providing us with necessary documentation, you help ensure that all debts are addressed according to legal standards, protecting both the estate and yourself from potential liability. If you have any questions or need further assistance with this process, please do not hesitate to contact our office.

Dealing with Creditor Claims in the Probate Process

During the administration of an estate, handling creditor claims properly is crucial to ensuring legal compliance and safeguarding the estate's assets. Here's what happens when a creditor claim is filed with the court and how these claims are processed:

Reviewing Creditor Claims

1. *Receipt of Claim:*

- Notification: When a creditor files a claim against the estate, the personal representative (you) will be notified. This claim will detail the amount owed and the basis of the debt.

2. *Evaluation of the Claim:*

- Assessment: You must review each creditor claim to determine its validity. This involves verifying that the debt existed and that the amount claimed is accurate.

Accepting or Rejecting Claims

1. *General Practice:*

- Acceptance: It is generally presumed that most creditor claims are valid, especially those substantiated by clear documentation such as contracts, invoices, or final bills.
- Preparation for Acceptance: We will prepare an acceptance document for you to sign for most claims, assuming they appear valid and are uncontested.

2. *Action on Accepted Claims:*

- Payment: Once a claim is accepted, it may be paid out of the estate's funds.
- Documentation: Always keep receipts or proof of payment for any claims paid. This is crucial for estate accounting and for reporting to the court.

3. REJECTING CLAIMS:

- Grounds for Rejection: If you believe a claim is incorrect, fraudulent, or otherwise invalid, you may choose to reject the claim.
- Notification: A formal notice of rejection must be sent to the creditor, who may then decide to contest the rejection in court.

Legal Implications

1. TIMELY RESPONSE REQUIRED:

- Statutory Deadlines: The law requires that the personal representative respond to creditor claims within a specific period (typically 30 days from the presentation of the claim).
- Consequences of Non-Response: Failure to respond can be construed as an acceptance of the claim.

2. DISPUTE RESOLUTION:

- Court Involvement: If a creditor disagrees with the rejection of their claim, they may petition the court for a resolution, which could lead to a hearing or settlement.

3. IMPACT ON ESTATE DISTRIBUTION:

- Payment Prioritization: Valid creditor claims must be paid before distributing the remaining assets to the heirs. This ensures that all debts are settled before the closure of the estate.

Conclusion

Handling creditor claims effectively is a key responsibility of the personal representative. It involves careful review, accurate record-keeping, and adherence to legal procedures. Proper management of these claims protects the estate from potential liabilities and ensures that the distribution of the estate's assets is conducted fairly and in accordance with the law. If you have any questions about a specific claim or need assistance with the claims process, please do not hesitate to contact our office for guidance.

Filing the Decedent's Final U.S. Individual Income Tax Return (IRS Form 1040)

When a person passes away, their tax obligations do not immediately cease. As the personal representative or executor, you are responsible for filing the decedent's final federal income tax return. Here is a detailed guide on what needs to be done:

Filing Requirements

1. *FINAL FORM 1040:*

- Due Date: The decedent's final Form 1040 must be filed by April 15 of the year following the decedent's death.
- Coverage: This tax return should include all income received and deductions eligible from January 1 to the date of death.

2. *FILING STATUS:*

- If the decedent was married at the time of death, the surviving spouse may file a joint return for the year of the decedent's death. This joint filing may include the income and deductions of the surviving spouse for the entire year.

3. *IDENTIFICATION ON THE FORM:*

- Mark the form as "Deceased," write the decedent's name, and the date of death across the top of the first page of Form 1040.

Tax Liabilities and Deductions

- Income Reporting: All income up to the date of death must be reported.
- Credits and Deductions: Claim all credits and deductions the decedent was entitled to. This includes personal exemptions and standard or itemized deductions.

Payment of Taxes

- Tax Due Date: Any income tax due must be paid by April 15 of the year following the year of death.
- Estate's Funds: The taxes due should ideally be paid from the estate's funds, as these are considered a liability of the estate.

Additional Considerations

1. *Prior Year Returns:*

- If the decedent had unfiled returns from previous years, those must also be filed by the executor to ensure compliance and prevent potential penalties.

2. *California State Income Tax Return (Form 540):*

- Similar rules apply for the state income tax return in California, with corresponding deadlines.

3. *Extensions and Audits:*

- Automatic Extension: An automatic 6-month extension to file can be obtained by submitting IRS Form 4868.
- Prompt Assessment: To hasten the closure of the estate, you can request a prompt assessment of the tax return, reducing

the audit period from three years to nine months using IRS Form 4810.

Stage 3G: Creditor Claims ™

Step	Tasks to Complete	What WE do	What YOU do	Estimated Time Frame
3H1	Hire a tax return Preparer	We can recommend a tax return preparer for you to	You hire a tax return preparer	After the Court issues Letters to You
3H2	Gather Information and Documents	We give you the Order for Probate, Letters, and Inventory and Appraisal	You work with the tax preparer to get the decedent's income tax information for the year of death and prior unfiled years from the IRS and FTB	After the Court issues Letters to You
3H3	Prepare and file federal and state income tax returns		You work with the tax preparer to prepare and file the decedent's income tax returns	After the Court issues Letters to You
3H4	Taxes Due and Refunds		You work with the tax preparer to pay any income taxes due or to request any refund owed	After the Court issues Letters to You

© 2024 ProbateDocs LLC

Documentation and IRS Communication

- Gathering Documentation: Compile financial records, previous tax returns, and bank statements to accurately prepare the final return.
- IRS Form 56: Notify the IRS of the fiduciary relationship using Form 56, which informs them that you are handling the decedent's tax matters.
- IRS Form 2848 and 8821: These forms allow you to appoint a tax professional to assist with tax matters and to access tax information from the IRS, respectively.

Important Steps

1. Review Past Filings: Ensure that at least the past three years of income tax returns were filed. If not, address this promptly.
2. Consult a Tax Professional: Given the complexities involved, consulting with a CPA or tax attorney is advisable to ensure all filings are accurate and timely.

Closing Note

Handling a decedent's final tax matters with diligence ensures compliance with tax laws and prevents personal liability issues for the estate's executor. If you need assistance or have questions about the process, consider reaching out to a professional experienced in estate and tax matters.

If It Is Taking More Than One Year for Estate Administration

The Probate Code allows for the personal representative to administer the estate for one year. If the estate administration will take longer than one year, then the personal representative is required to file an accounting for each year of administration. Alternatively, the personal representative can file a status report of the administration over the prior year. The status report would report the actions taken over the prior year, what more work is needed to complete the estate administration, and an estimate of how much longer the personal representative needs to complete the estate administration.

Requirements for Filing an Accounting or Status Report in Probate Cases

Managing a probate case involves adhering to specific timelines set by the Probate Code to ensure timely and efficient administration of the estate. Here is a detailed explanation of the requirements for filing an accounting or a status report if the probate case extends beyond one year from the issuance of Letters to the personal representative.

Timeline for Closing a Probate Case

- **One-Year Expectation:** The Probate Code generally expects that a probate case will be completed within one year from when the personal representative receives Letters (the official document authorizing them to act on behalf of the estate).

Filing Requirements After One Year

1. ACCOUNTING OR STATUS REPORT:

- **Mandatory Filing:** If the probate case is not ready to be closed within one year, the personal representative is required to file either an accounting or a status report with the probate court.
- **Purpose:** This document should explain the current status of estate administration, what remains to be done, and an estimated timeline for completion.

2. CONTENT OF THE STATUS REPORT:

- **Details Required:** The status report must detail the reasons why the estate is not yet settled and provide a projected timeline for finalizing the administration.
- **Annual Requirement:** A status report must be submitted annually as long as the probate matter remains open.

3. COURT APPROVAL:

- **Filing Fee:** Submitting a status report or accounting requires a filing fee.
- **Court Order:** The court must approve the continued

administration of the estate beyond one year, and similarly for each successive year the case remains open.

Stage 31: Account or Status Report ™

Step	Tasks to Complete	What WE do	What YOU do	Estimated Time Frame
311	Gather Information and Documents	We email You a Questionnaire to fill out electronically	You fill out the Questionnaire and email documents to Us	One year from when the Court issues Letters to You
312	Review of Information and Documents	We review the Questionnaire and documents, You provide information or documents needed	You respond with any information or documents, if needed	Time varies, with complexity of Your case and when You gather information and documents
313	Drafting the Status Report	We draft the Status Report	You review and sign the Status Report	Within three business days of having all information and documents needed
314	File the Status Report with the Court	We file the Status Report with the Court (We pay the court fees and eFile fee from Your deposit)		Processing times may vary as the Court may take some time to process and schedule the court hearing
315	Mail Notice of the Status Report Court Hearing	We mail Notice of the Status Report Court Hearing to Everyone		At least 30 days prior to the court hearing
316	Court Hearing and Order	We attend the court hearing and get the Court Order - (We pay the eFiling fee from Your deposit)	You are not required to attend the court hearing, but You can attend if You want to	Processing times may vary as the Court may take some time to process

© 2024 ProbateDocs LLC

Role of Heirs

- Demand for Accounting: Any heir to the estate has the right to request that the personal representative file a formal accounting with the court, which provides a detailed financial record of the estate's management.

Consequences of Delay

- Sanctions or Removal: If the personal representative fails to administer the estate efficiently and within a reasonable timeframe, the court has the authority to impose sanctions or remove the personal representative for failing to fulfill their duties.

Associated Costs

1. Probate Bond Premiums:

- Annual Premiums: If the administration of the estate extends beyond one year, the bond company will bill the personal representative directly for the annual premium.
- Payment Responsibility: If there are insufficient funds in the estate's account to cover the bond premium, the personal representative must pay out of their own pocket.
- Refunds: After the first year's premium, any subsequent premiums may be refundable for any unused portion upon exoneration of the bond.

2. Exoneration of the Bond:

- Final Discharge: The bond is only canceled once the Ex Parte Petition for Final Discharge is issued by the court after all funds have been disbursed and receipts filed.

Final Steps

- Court Processing Times: Be aware that processing times by the court can vary, which may affect the timeline for closing the estate.

Summary

Filing an accounting or a status report if a probate case extends beyond the expected one-year timeframe is critical for maintaining transparency with the court and the heirs, and for fulfilling the responsibilities as a personal representative. It's essential to stay proactive in managing the estate and to communicate effectively with all parties involved to avoid potential legal complications.

Ancillary Probate

Ancillary probate is required when a decedent owns property in a state different from their domicile at the time of death. It serves to handle the legal aspects of the property located outside the primary probate jurisdiction.

Key Points of Ancillary Probate

1. Jurisdiction and Domicile:

- Probate is typically initiated in the state where the decedent was domiciled (officially resided with intent to remain).
- Ancillary probate handles property in any other state or country where the decedent owned property.

2. Property Management:

- Each state has jurisdiction over tangible property located within its borders at the time of the owner's death.
- The laws of the state where the property is located usually govern the distribution of that property.

3. California-Specific Rules:

- In California, ancillary administration is necessary when a non-domiciliary decedent owns property within the state.
- A California personal representative must notify known creditors in other jurisdictions.

4. REAL PROPERTY AND ESTATE ADMINISTRATION:

- Real property (like land or buildings) located outside of California requires ancillary probate in the state where the property is situated.
- Ancillary probate in California treats the estate as if the decedent were domiciled in California, following similar procedures and allowing for similar compensation for personal representatives and attorneys.

5. CREDITOR CLAIMS AND NOTIFICATIONS:

- Known creditors must be notified according to the specific requirements of the state handling the ancillary probate.

6. SPECIAL CONSIDERATIONS FOR CALIFORNIA:

- If a non-California resident's personal property in California is valued under $184,500, it may be collected through an affidavit procedure, avoiding formal probate.
- Ancillary probate in California involves filing a modified Petition for Probate to accommodate non-domiciliary statuses and ensuring all international protocols (like obtaining an apostille for foreign documents under the Hague Convention) are followed.

7. HANDLING MULTIPLE JURISDICTIONS:

- When assets are located in multiple jurisdictions, the rules of each state concerning estate administration, creditor notifications, and property transfers apply.
- Venue for ancillary probate is usually determined by the location of the property.

By understanding these key elements, personal representatives can navigate the complexities of managing an estate that spans multiple legal jurisdictions effectively. Ancillary probate ensures that all property is appropriately handled according to the respective laws of each state or country involved, providing a clear legal path to settle all aspects of an individual's estate.

Stage 3J: Ancillary Probate ™

Step	Tasks to Complete	What WE do	What YOU do	Estimated Time Frame
3J1	Identify Assets in Another State	We email You a Questionnaire to fill out electronically	You fill out the Questionnaire and email documents to Us	After you are appointed as the personal representative
3J2	Review of Information and Documents	We review the Questionnaire and documents, You provide information or documents as needed	You respond with any information or documents, if needed	Time varies, with complexity of Your case and when You gather information and documents
3J3	Hire Attorney in Another State	We may be able to refer an attorney in another state to You	You hire an attorney in another state to handle the ancillary probate	After you are appointed as the personal representative
3J4	Complete the Ancillary Probate	We file the Status Report with the Court (We pay the court fees and eFile fee from Your deposit)		Processing times may vary as the Court may take some time to process and schedule the court hearing
3J5	Mail Notice of the Status Report Court Hearing	We mail Notice of the Status Report Court Hearing to Everyone		At least 30 days prior to the court hearing
3J6	Court Hearing and Order	We attend the court hearing and get the Court Order - (We pay the eFiling fee from Your deposit)	You are not required to attend the court hearing, but You can attend if You want to	Processing times may vary as the Court may take some time to process

© 2024 ProbateDocs LLC

STAGE 4
WINDING DOWN THE ESTATE ™

Stage 4: Winding Down the Estate™ represents a transitional phase in the probate process where the primary focus shifts from active management of the estate's assets to preparing for their distribution. This stage involves compiling all necessary documentation, addressing any remaining financial matters, and submitting the final petition to the court. It serves as the precursor to officially closing the estate and distributing assets to the beneficiaries.

Key Components of Stage 4

1. Final Accounting or Waiver Thereof

- Preparation of an Accounting: If required, the personal representative prepares a detailed accounting report for the court. This report itemizes all financial transactions made during the estate administration, including income received, expenses paid, and the sale of assets. The accounting provides a transparent record that ensures all actions taken have been in the best interest of the estate.
- Waiver of Accounting: In some cases, all heirs may agree to waive the formal accounting process. This can simplify proceedings and reduce costs, but it requires the unanimous consent of all heirs.

2. Drafting the Final Petition

- Report to the Court: The final petition includes a comprehensive report that summarizes the actions taken during the estate administration and proposes how the remaining assets should be distributed according to the will or state law.
- Proposed Distribution: The petition outlines the proposed distribution of assets to the heirs and beneficiaries. This includes specific bequests outlined in the will and the division of the residuary estate.

3. Clearing Remaining Financial Obligations

- Settlement of Final Debts and Expenses: Before the estate can be closed, all outstanding debts, taxes, and administrative expenses must be settled. This ensures that the estate is free of liabilities before assets are distributed.
- Reserve for Uncertain Costs: Sometimes, a reserve fund is retained to cover unforeseen expenses or late-arriving claims. The size and necessity of this reserve are typically dictated by the complexity of the estate and any potential financial uncertainties.

Triggering Event for Moving to Stage 5

The completion and filing of the Final Petition with the probate court mark the transition to the next stage. The court will review the petition and set a hearing date to address any issues and approve the proposed actions.

Moving to Stage 5 – Petitioning for the Final Order™ involves publicizing the hearing date to all interested parties, addressing any final probate notes or objections from the court, and attending the court hearing. The approval of the Final Petition and issuance of the Final Order by the judge are critical steps that authorize the personal representative to distribute the estate's assets and ultimately close the probate case.

Winding Down the Estate is crucial for ensuring that all legal and financial requirements have been met before the estate is closed. It provides a clear pathway for the seamless transition to asset distribution and the final discharge of the personal representative's duties.

Stage 4: Winding Down the Estate ™

Step 4a: Gather Information and Documents

You give Us information and documents

Step 4b: Review of Information and Documents

- Not All Heirs Waive an Account → **Step 4c: Draft Final Petition with Account**
- All Heirs Waive an Account → **Step 4c: Draft Final Petition with Waiver of Account**

Step 4d: Review and Sign the Final Petition

We receive your signed Petition for Probate

Step 4e: Deposit for Fees and Costs

We deposit funds in Our Client Trust Account

Step 4f: File Final Petition with the Court

The Court sets a court hearing date

© 2024 ProbateDocs LLC

Stage 4: Winding Down the Estate ™

Step	Tasks to Complete	What WE do	What YOU do	Estimated Time Frame
4a	Gather Information and Documents	After estate administration is completed, We email you a Questionnaire to fill out	You fill out the Questionnaire and email Us copies of bank statements	Must be at least four months from issuance of Letters
4b	Review of Information and Documents	We review the Questionnaire and documents, You provide information or documents needed	You respond with any information or documents, if needed	Time varies, with complexity of Your case and when You gather information and documents
4c	Drafting the Final Petition, and Accounting If Needed	We draft the Final Petition and an Accounting, if needed		Within five business days of having all information and documents needed
4d	Review and Sign the Final Petition	We email You the Final Petition and Proposed Estimated Distribution to sign electronically	You review and sign the Final Petition and Proposed Estimated Distribution - Inform Us of any changes	We will contact You when We send to You to sign
4e	Deposit for Fees and Costs	We deposit the attorney fees and costs in Our client trust account	You overnight mail Us a check for the attorney fees and costs	Time varies, with when We receive the funds
4f	File the Final Petition with the Court	We file the Final Petition with the Court (We pay the court filing fee and eFiling fee from Your deposit)		Processing times may vary as the Court may take some time to process

© 2024 ProbateDocs LLC

Winding Down the Estate After Administration Completion

Once all aspects of estate administration are completed, the process to formally close the estate begins. This involves several key steps to ensure everything is finalized according to legal standards. Here's a detailed breakdown of how we will proceed with winding down the estate:

Steps to Wind Down the Estate

1. *GATHERING INFORMATION AND DOCUMENTS:*

- From You: We will need to collect all pertinent information and documents from you that relate to the estate's administration. This includes financial records, receipts, and documentation of assets and liabilities handled during the administration phase.

2. *PREPARATION OF LEGAL DOCUMENTS:*

- Petition and Accounting: We will draft the final petition for the closure of the estate and prepare an accounting if required by the court. The accounting will detail all financial transactions made during the administration of the estate.

3. *FUNDING FOR LEGAL FEES AND COSTS:*

- Deposit Requirement: You will need to provide a deposit from the estate's funds to cover our legal fees and the costs associated with filing the petition. This deposit will be held in our client trust account until used for estate-related expenses.

4. *FILING THE PETITION:*

- Court Filing: We will file the prepared petition with the probate court, which will then set a date for a court hearing.
- Notice of Hearing: Notice of the court hearing will be mailed out to all interested parties, including heirs and creditors, to inform them of when and where the hearing will take place.

5. *ADDRESSING COURT INQUIRIES:*

- Probate Notes: The court may issue probate notes that require responses to clarify or correct information in the petition. We can address these inquiries with a supplement that you will need to sign.

6. *Court Hearing:*

- Attendance: We will attend the court hearing on your behalf; your presence at the hearing is not mandatory but you are welcome to attend if you wish.
- Court Approval: At the hearing, the judge will review the petition and the accounting, and if everything is in order, approve the closing of the estate.

After the Court Hearing

- Distribution of Assets: Once the court approves the petition, the final distribution of the estate's assets can proceed according to the decedent's will or state law if there is no will.
- Final Disbursements: Any remaining payments, including those to creditors, heirs, and any administrative fees, will be made.
- Closing Statements: We will prepare final closing statements for the estate, which detail all distributions and the closure of the estate accounts.

Conclusion

Winding down an estate is the final step in the probate process and requires careful preparation and coordination. It is the culmination of all the administrative work performed post-death and ensures that all legal and financial obligations have been met. If you have any questions about this process or need further assistance, please do not hesitate to contact our office.

Understanding an Accounting in the Probate Process

An accounting in the context of probate is a detailed financial report that provides transparency and accountability for the management of a decedent's estate. Here's what you need to know about the accounting process:

Purpose of an Accounting

An accounting serves several key purposes within the probate process:

- Transparency: It provides a clear and detailed record of all financial transactions that have occurred within the estate.
- Accountability: It holds the personal representative responsible for their handling of the estate's assets and liabilities.
- Clarity for Beneficiaries: It ensures that all parties interested in the estate, particularly the heirs, have a comprehensive understanding of the financial activities and the current status of the estate's assets.

Components of an Accounting

An accounting typically includes the following elements:

- Assets Marshaled: A list of all assets that were collected and brought under the control of the estate.
- Income Received: All forms of income that the estate received, such as rents, dividends, interest, or other forms of earnings.
- Expenses and Disbursements: All money that was paid out from the estate, including debts, taxes, administrative expenses, and distributions to heirs.
- Remaining Assets: A summary of what assets remain in the estate after all income has been collected and expenses have been paid.

Requirement for an Accounting

- Mandatory vs. Waiver: In most cases, an accounting is required to be filed with the probate court. However, this requirement can be waived if all heirs to the estate agree to forego the accounting. A waiver typically occurs when heirs trust the executor's management and wish to avoid the formality and expense of a formal accounting.

Filing an Accounting

- Court Review: Once submitted, the accounting is reviewed by the probate court to ensure it is complete and accurate.
- Approval: Approval of the accounting by the court is necessary before the estate can be closed and any remaining assets distributed according to the decedent's will or state law.

Importance of Accuracy

- Legal and Financial Implications: Accuracy in the accounting is crucial as errors can lead to disputes among heirs, potential legal challenges, or even charges of mismanagement against the executor.

Conclusion

An accounting is an essential part of the estate administration process, providing a detailed record of the financial management of the estate. It ensures that the personal representative has properly accounted for the assets entrusted to them and clarifies the state of the estate's finances for all interested parties. If you have any questions or need assistance with preparing an accounting for the estate, please contact our office. We are here to help ensure that all financial aspects of the estate are handled with the utmost care and professionalism.

Understanding a Waiver of Accounting in Probate

In probate proceedings, an accounting is typically required to provide a detailed report of the financial management of the estate to the court and all interested parties. However, there is an option to waive this requirement if all heirs agree.

What is a Waiver of Accounting?

A waiver of accounting is a formal agreement in which all heirs to an estate agree not to require the personal representative to file a detailed accounting of the estate's financial transactions with the probate court. This can simplify the probate process and reduce costs associated with preparing and filing detailed reports.

Process for Obtaining a Waiver of Accounting

1. *CONSENT OF ALL HEIRS:*

- All heirs must agree to waive the accounting requirement. This consent must be given in writing to ensure it is legally binding.

2. *DOCUMENTATION:*

- Waiver Form: We will prepare an accounting waiver form that details the decision to waive the formal accounting. This form needs to be signed by all heirs.
- Electronic Signatures: To facilitate the process, we can send this waiver form for electronic signatures, ensuring that all parties can conveniently sign the document, even if they are in different locations.

Submissions to the Court Despite the Waiver

Even if an accounting is waived, there are still minimal requirements to ensure transparency and accountability:

1. ESTATE BANK ACCOUNT STATEMENTS:

- Copies of the estate's bank account statements must still be submitted to the court. These provide a basic overview of the financial transactions handled by the estate.

2. REAL ESTATE CLOSING STATEMENTS:

- If real estate properties were sold during the administration of the estate, the closing statements from these transactions must be provided to the court.

3. RECEIPTS FOR REIMBURSEMENTS:

- If you, as the personal representative, are requesting reimbursements for expenses paid out-of-pocket on behalf of the estate, receipts for these expenses must be submitted. This ensures that all disbursements are accounted for and justified.

Legal Implications

- Simplifies the Probate Process: Waiving the detailed accounting can streamline the closure of the estate, making it quicker and less costly.
- Responsibility Remains: Despite the waiver, the personal representative is still responsible for handling the estate's assets prudently and transparently. The waiver primarily affects the level of detail required in reporting to the court, not the underlying duty to manage the estate responsibly.

Conclusion

Obtaining a waiver of accounting can be beneficial for all parties involved by simplifying the administrative process and reducing related costs. However, it is crucial to ensure that all heirs are in agreement and that essential financial documents are still provided to fulfill legal requirements and maintain transparency. If you decide to proceed with a waiver of accounting, we will assist in preparing all necessary documentation and ensuring that all minimal legal submissions are made to the court.

Understanding Statutory Commission and Taxation of Personal Representative Fees

As the personal representative (also known as the executor) of an estate, you play a crucial role in managing and finalizing the estate's affairs. For your services, you are entitled to compensation, which is regulated by statutory laws. Here's an explanation of the statutory commission you may receive, and the tax implications associated with it.

Statutory Commission

The statutory commission is the fee you are entitled to as the personal representative, based on a percentage of the value of the estate you are administering. This fee compensates you for the time and effort spent managing the estate, and it is determined by state laws. Typically, the commission is calculated as a percentage of the total assets that come into your hands as the personal representative.

Required Documentation for Accounting

To accurately calculate your statutory commission, it is essential to have detailed records of all estate transactions:

1. *Bank Statements:*

- Decedent's Bank Account: Provide all pages, front and back, from the date of death until all funds are withdrawn, and the account is closed.
- Estate Bank Account: Include all pages, front and back, from the date the account was opened up to the most current month.

2. *Transaction Details:*

- Include a description of any checks or withdrawals from the estate bank account to validate the disbursements made under your administration.

3. *Real Estate Transactions:*

- Provide all real estate closing statements if property sales occurred during the estate administration. These are vital for determining the total asset value managed.

Taxation of Personal Representative Fee

It's important to understand the tax implications of your compensation:

- Taxable Income: Unlike inheritance, which generally isn't taxable, the fee you receive as a personal representative is taxable income. You will need to report this income on your personal tax return.
- Gains from Estate Assets: Any gains realized from the sale of estate assets during administration (e.g., real estate sold at a profit) are also subject to taxation.

Filing Requirements

To ensure compliance with tax laws and proper reporting:

- Include your personal representative fee as income on your IRS Form 1040.
- If the estate sells assets and realizes gains, these must be reported appropriately, usually through the estate's tax return, and could affect the estate's tax liabilities.

Conclusion

Managing an estate is a responsibility that comes with both compensation and obligations. Understanding your entitlements under statutory commissions and the associated tax requirements helps in effectively managing both the estate's and your financial responsibilities. If you have any questions about the documentation required for the accounting or the taxation of your personal representative fee, please feel free to contact our office for further guidance.

Reimbursement for Administrative Expenses in Estate Administration

As the personal representative of an estate, you may incur various expenses that are necessary for managing and settling the estate. It's important to understand which expenses are reimbursable by the estate and what you need to do to request reimbursement from the probate court.

What is Reimbursable?

You can be reimbursed for out-of-pocket expenses that are necessary for the administration of the estate, including:

1. *Probate Court or Case Fees*: Any filing fees or costs associated directly with the probate case.

2. *Real Estate Maintenance Costs*:
- Mortgage payments, if they are necessary to prevent foreclosure.

- Property taxes to avoid penalties and interest.
- Utilities to maintain the property in good condition.
- Repairs and maintenance that are essential to preserve the value of the property.

3. *Travel Expenses*:

- A short trip (including flight, hotel, and car rental) that is necessary for you to manage or secure estate assets.

What is NOT Reimbursable?

Certain expenses are generally not reimbursable because they are considered part of the personal responsibility or are deemed unreasonable for estate purposes:

1. GENERAL ADMINISTRATIVE COSTS:

- Mailing costs.
- Telephone charges.
- Food costs during trips or meetings related to the estate.

2. TRAVEL:

- Mileage or gas for local travel.
- Any additional travel not directly necessary for estate administration.

3. LABOR COSTS:

- Your personal labor costs for managing the estate.

4. UNREASONABLE OR UNNECESSARY EXPENSES:

- Any expenses that the judge deems excessive or not directly related to estate management.

Requesting Reimbursement

To request reimbursement from the estate for out-of-pocket expenses, please follow these steps:

1. Documentation:

- Gather receipts or invoices for all expenses you are claiming.
- Make a list of each expense, including the date, payee, description, and amount. This helps in the verification and approval process by the court.

2. Submit to Us:

- Provide all these documents to our office. We will review them to ensure they meet the criteria for reimbursable expenses and prepare the necessary documentation to submit to the probate court.

3. Court Approval:

- We will file a petition or request with the probate court to approve your reimbursements. The court may require additional information or clarification before approving the expenses.

Importance of Compliance

It is crucial to comply with these guidelines to ensure that you are reimbursed for eligible expenses and that the estate's resources are used appropriately. Unapproved or personal expenses could lead to disputes or challenges from heirs or beneficiaries, and potentially, disapproval by the court.

Please gather the necessary documentation for any expenses you believe are reimbursable and provide them to our office as soon as possible. If you have any questions about what constitutes a reimbursable expense or need help organizing your receipts, feel free to reach out. We're here to help you manage the estate efficiently and effectively.

Statutory Commissions for Ordinary Services

When it comes to calculating statutory commissions for ordinary services in a probate case, attorneys and personal representatives are entitled to compensation based on the total gross value of the estate. The fees are calculated using the appraised value of all estate assets, adjusted for receipts, gains on sales, and net business income, minus any losses from sales or business activities.

Calculating the Statutory Commissions

Here's how the attorney's statutory commission for ordinary services is typically structured:

1. *Fee Base Calculation:*

- Inventory and Appraisal Value: Start with the total value of all estate assets as appraised.
- Additions: Include all receipts, gains on sales of assets, and net income generated by any businesses included in the estate.
- Subtractions: Subtract losses from sales and any losses from business operations.
- The result is the Fee Base on which the statutory fees are calculated.

2. *Percentage Scale:*

- 4% on the first $100,000 of the estate's value.
- 3% on the next $100,000.
- 2% on any amount between $200,000 and $1,000,000.
- 1% on any amount between $1,000,000 and $10,000,000.
- For estates valued over $10,000,000, the percentage might vary based on local laws and specific court orders.

Example of Statutory Commission Calculations

Example Calculation:

- For an estate valued at $500,000:
- $4,000 (4% of the first $100,000)
- $3,000 (3% of the next $100,000)
- $6,000 (2% of the remaining $300,000)
- Total fee = $13,000

These fees compensate the attorney and the personal representative for their work in managing and closing the estate. It's important to note that these fees are taken from the estate before distribution to heirs or beneficiaries. This remuneration recognizes the responsibility, expertise, and time required to properly administer an estate, ensuring that all legal, financial, and tax-related matters are handled according to the law.

If you have any specific questions about the fees or need a detailed breakdown based on the specific assets in the estate, feel free to ask, and we can provide more personalized information.

Extraordinary Fees for Extraordinary Services

Extraordinary fees in a probate case are charged for services that go beyond the standard duties involved in managing and closing an estate. These services are typically billed on an hourly basis, and must be specifically approved by the court due to their nature exceeding regular probate work.

Definition and Examples of Extraordinary Services

- Litigation: If there are disputes that require legal resolution, such as will contests, disputes among heirs, or claims against the estate that result in court proceedings.
- Complex Asset Transactions: Involvement in the sale of estate assets that require significant legal oversight beyond routine transactions, such as the sale of real estate, transferring

business interests, or handling unique or valuable collectibles that might require negotiations or specialized knowledge.
- Tax Issues: Handling complex tax matters such as filing estate taxes, negotiating with tax authorities, or dealing with audits can qualify as extraordinary services.
- Specialized Advice: Providing specialized advice or services relating to the valuation of unusual assets, establishing and managing trusts, or international aspects of the estate.

Approval and Payment of Extraordinary Fees

- Court Approval: These fees must be documented in detail and submitted to the probate court for approval. This is to ensure that the fees are justified and directly related to the services provided.
- Separate Accounting: Fees for extraordinary services must be tracked separately from the standard statutory fees to clearly delineate ordinary probate administration from the additional tasks performed.
- Reasonableness: The court will review the reasonableness of the fees based on the complexity of the services, the amount of time spent, and the customary fees for such services in the legal community.

For example, if we engage in litigation to defend the estate in a contest over the will, or if we are involved in the detailed negotiation and sale of a complex asset like commercial real estate or a part of the decedent's business, these would be billed as extraordinary services. These fees are in addition to the regular statutory fees calculated based on the value of the estate's assets.

It is important for you, as the personal representative, to understand these potential additional costs and to communicate with us openly about any complex issues that might arise during the administration of the estate. If you anticipate any such scenarios, please discuss them with us early in the process so we can plan accordingly and ensure proper court approval for any extraordinary services required.

Deposit for Fees and Costs

As we prepare to finalize the closure of the estate, we will need to ensure all necessary legal and financial obligations are completed. This includes preparing and filing the final petition to close out the estate. At this stage, we will ask you for a deposit to cover our statutory commissions and any extraordinary fees, as well as the anticipated closing expenses.

Here's what this entails

1. Statutory Commissions and Extraordinary Fees: These are calculated based on the services provided throughout the administration of the estate. Statutory commissions are calculated based on the total value of the estate's assets, and extraordinary fees are charged for any legal work that goes beyond routine probate tasks.

2. Estimated Closing Expenses: This includes:

- Court Filing Fees: To file the final petition and other necessary documents with the probate court.
- Conformed Copy of the Court Order: We will obtain a conformed copy of the court order which is a certified copy showing that it has been filed and approved by the court.
- Filing of the Conformed Court Order for Real Estate Transfers: If the estate includes real property, a copy of the conformed court order may need to be filed with the county recorder's office to finalize the transfer of the property to the heirs or new owners.

Importance of the Deposit:

- The deposit ensures that there are sufficient funds to cover the costs of completing the probate process without delay.
- It allows us to efficiently manage the remaining tasks and ensures that all financial obligations are met promptly as required by the court.

Procedure:

- Upon receiving your deposit, we will proceed with drafting and filing the final petition.
- We will handle all necessary court filings and ensure that every step is taken to comply with probate laws and court requirements.
- You will be kept informed of the status and notified of the court hearing date and any further requirements or probate notes from the court.

It is essential to address these financial aspects as we approach the final stages of the estate's administration to ensure a smooth and successful closure. If you have any questions about the deposit or the fees and expenses involved, please do not hesitate to contact us. We are here to assist you through every step of this process.

As we approach the final stages of administering the estate, it's essential to prepare for filing the final petition to close the estate. Here's what you need to know, and the steps involved:

Steps to File the Final Petition

1. Creditor Claim Period: At least four months must have passed since the issuance of the "letters" (authority granted to you as the personal representative).

2. Administration Completion: You should have completed all the necessary administration tasks for the estate.

3. Estate Bank Statements: Ensure all bank statements related to the estate have been sent to our office. These documents are critical for finalizing the accounts.

4. Deposit for Fees and Costs: You need to provide a deposit covering our attorney fees and any other related costs to proceed with the closing of the estate.

Accounting or Waiver of Accounting

- Waiver of Accounting: If all heirs agree, they can sign a waiver to forgo a formal accounting, which simplifies the closing process. We will prepare the necessary documents for the waiver.
- Requirement of Accounting: If not all heirs agree to waive the accounting, as a personal representative, you must prepare a detailed accounting of all estate transactions. This includes:
- A simple accounting handled by us for straightforward estates.
- A complex accounting, which may require a professional accountant if the estate's financial matters are more intricate.

Options for the Final Petition

- Statutory Fee: Consider if you want to claim your statutory fee for ordinary services. This fee is taxable income.
- Extraordinary Fee: If you performed tasks beyond the ordinary duties (like selling real estate), you might be eligible for extraordinary fees. You'll need detailed records of the work done to submit for court approval.
- Reimbursable Expenses: Submit any out-of-pocket expenses you've incurred while administering the estate for reimbursement. Not all expenses may be reimbursable, and they need judicial approval.

Next Steps

1. *Gather and Submit Documentation*: Compile all necessary documents, including bank statements and receipts for expenses.
2. *Decision on Fees and Reimbursements*: Decide whether you will claim your statutory and extraordinary fees, and which expenses you wish to be reimbursed for.
3. *Contact Us*: Once you have gathered the information and made decisions regarding fees and reimbursements, please

contact our office. We will assist in preparing the final petition and ensure that all your submissions are in order.

This procedure ensures that the estate is closed properly and in accordance with legal standards, allowing for a clear and uncontested distribution of the estate's assets to the heirs. If you have any questions or need further clarification on any of these points, please don't hesitate to reach out.

STAGE 5
PETITIONING FOR THE FINAL ORDER

Stage 5: Petitioning for the Final Order™ marks a critical phase in the probate process where the preparation and submission efforts culminate in a court hearing to obtain judicial approval for the final distribution of the estate's assets. This stage is pivotal as it seeks to resolve any remaining issues and secure a court order that authorizes the execution of the final steps in the estate closure.

Key Components of Stage 5

1. Notice of Hearing

- Mailing Notices: Once the Final Petition is filed and the court hearing date is set, the personal representative is responsible for mailing notices to all interested parties, including all heirs, beneficiaries, and creditors who have shown interest in the estate. This ensures that all parties are informed and have the opportunity to attend the hearing or file objections.
- Publication Requirements: In some cases, especially when there are unknown creditors or interested parties, the law may require the notice of the hearing to be published in a local newspaper. This step is crucial for satisfying legal requirements for transparency and public notification.

2. Addressing Probate Notes

- Clarifications and Corrections: Prior to the hearing, the court may issue probate notes—queries or requests for clarification on the Final Petition. The personal representative must address these notes, often by submitting additional documents or amendments to the court, to clear up any issues that might prevent the order from being granted.

3. Court Hearing

- Attendance and Testimony: The personal representative, often accompanied by their attorney, must attend the court hearing. During this hearing, they may need to testify about the estate and the actions taken during its administration. This is also an opportunity for other parties to raise any last-minute concerns or objections to the distribution plan or other elements of the Final Petition.

4. Judicial Approval and Final Order

- Judge's Review: The judge reviews all the materials and testimonies provided to ensure that the estate has been managed appropriately and that the proposed distribution is just and in accordance with the law.
- Issuance of the Final Order: If satisfied, the judge will issue a Final Order for distribution. This legally binding document authorizes the personal representative to distribute the estate's assets according to the terms outlined in the Final Petition.

Triggering Event for Moving to Stage 6

The issuance of the Final Order by the court is the triggering event that moves the probate case to its final stage, Stage 6: Distribution and Discharge™. Once the order is received, the personal representative can proceed with distributing the assets as specified, paying any last-minute administrative costs, and ultimately seeking to be discharged from their role.

Moving to Stage 6 - Distribution and Discharge™ involves the actual handover of estate assets to the heirs and beneficiaries, filing of final tax returns, settling any outstanding administrative expenses, and submitting an Ex Parte Petition for Final Discharge to the court. This stage finalizes the probate process, ensuring that all responsibilities are completed, and the personal representative's duties are formally concluded.

Stage 5: Court Issues Final Order ™

- **Step 5a: Mail Notice**
  - Send notice 15 days before the court hearing
- **Step 5b: Review Probate Notes**
  - We review the probate notes
- **Step 5c: Draft a Supplement to Clear Probate Notes**
  - You Review and Sign the Supplement
- **Step 5d: Attend the Court Hearing**
  - The Final Petition is Approved

© 2024 ProbateDocs LLC

137

Stage 5: Court Issues Final Order ™

Step	Tasks to Complete	What WE do	What YOU do	Estimated Time Frame
5a	Mail Notice	We mail a notice of the Final Petition (We pay the eFiling fee from Your deposit)		Mailed at least 15 days before the court hearing
5b	Review Probate Notes	We review the court's Probate Notes, and ask for any additional information or documents needed	You respond with any information or documents, if needed	Time varies, with complexity of Your case and when You gather information and documents
5c	Draft a Supplement to Clear Probate Notes	We draft a Supplement to clear the Probate Notes (We pay the eFiling fee from Your deposit)	You review and sign the Supplement - Inform Us of any changes	Completed within two business days once we have Your information and documents
5d	Court Hearing	We attend the court hearing, and the judge signs the Order for Distribution (We pay the conformed copy fee and eFiling fee from Your deposit)	You are not required to attend the court hearing, but You can attend if You want to	Our hearing will be very short, but We may have to wait for other hearings - It may take time for the court to process the Order

© 2024 ProbateDocs LLC

The Final Petition and Court Hearing

Filing the final petition is a critical step in the probate process, marking the transition towards closing the estate. Here's how this stage will unfold:

Drafting and Filing the Final Petition

Once all necessary documentation and information are compiled, including account statements and any required receipts or waivers:

1. *Drafting the Petition*: Our office will prepare the final petition, detailing the actions taken during the administration of the estate and the proposed distribution of assets.
2. *Your Review and Signature*: We will send the drafted petition

to you for review. Once you've signed it, confirming that all the details are correct and complete, we will proceed to file it with the probate court.

Court Process

3. *Court Hearing Date*: After filing, the court will schedule a hearing. The timing for this depends on the court's schedule, which can vary significantly.
4. *Notice of Hearing*: We will send notices to all interested parties, informing them of the upcoming court hearing as required by law. This ensures all beneficiaries and potential claimants are aware and have the opportunity to attend or contest the petition if they choose.

Judge's Approval and Order

5. *Court Hearing*: The hearing is an opportunity for the court to review the petition and ensure that the estate has been managed properly. We will represent you during this hearing, addressing any questions the court might have.
6. *Judge's Approval*: If the court is satisfied with the petition and there are no objections, the judge will approve the petition and sign the final order for distribution.

Final Steps of the Estate

7. *Distribution and Discharge*: Following the judge's approval, we will execute the distribution of the estate's assets according to the terms of the will (if one exists) or the law (if there is no will). This involves transferring assets to the beneficiaries, settling any remaining expenses, and ensuring all administrative tasks are completed.
8. *Final Discharge*: Once all distributions have been made and confirmed, we will file for a final discharge from the

court, relieving you of further responsibilities as the personal representative.

This process officially concludes the probate proceedings, effectively closing out the estate and releasing you from your duties. If you have any concerns or need further clarification as we prepare to undertake these steps, please don't hesitate to reach out. We're here to ensure everything proceeds smoothly and to address any of your questions along the way.

STAGE 6
DISTRIBUTION AND DISCHARGE ™

Stage 6: Distribution and Discharge™ is the final phase in the probate process where the personal representative distributes the estate's assets to the rightful heirs and beneficiaries and completes all administrative tasks to close the estate. This stage ensures that all the directives in the Final Order are carried out and that the personal representative is officially relieved from their duties by the court.

Key Components of Stage 6

1. Distributing Assets

- Execution of the Final Order: The personal representative follows the directives specified in the Final Order to distribute the estate's assets. This might include transferring titles, disbursing funds, or handling specific bequests as stipulated in the will or determined by the court.
- Issuing Receipts: Each heir or beneficiary is required to sign a receipt when they receive their portion of the estate. This serves as proof of delivery and acceptance of their inheritance, which protects the personal representative from future claims or disputes.

2. Handling Final Administrative Tasks

- Paying Final Expenses: The personal representative ensures that all remaining expenses related to the estate are settled.

This includes paying any outstanding bills, final probate court fees, and costs associated with the transfer of property.
- Filing Final Tax Returns: This includes both the estate's income tax return and any final personal tax returns on behalf of the decedent, ensuring all tax obligations are met to avoid penalties or audits.

3. Ex Parte Petition for Final Discharge

- Filing for Discharge: After distributing all assets and completing all tasks, the personal representative files an Ex Parte Petition for Final Discharge with the court. This petition requests the court to officially release the personal representative from their duties, marking the formal conclusion of their role.
- Court Review and Approval: The court reviews the petition along with all accompanying receipts and final accountings. If satisfied, the judge will issue an order granting the discharge, legally freeing the personal representative from any further responsibilities associated with the estate.

4. Exonerating the Probate Bond

- Notifying the Bond Company: Once the final discharge is granted, it is crucial to inform the bond company so that the probate bond can be canceled or exonerated. This releases the personal representative and the estate from the bond obligation, preventing any future claims against it.

5. Resolving Remaining Funds

- Managing Reserve Funds: If there were reserve funds kept back to cover unforeseen expenses or late-arriving bills, the personal representative must ensure these are properly allocated. This may involve paying supplemental property tax bills, covering costs for filing the estate's final tax return, or other approved expenses.

- Closing Accounts: Finally, any remaining estate accounts are closed, and if there are any residual funds after covering all expenses and distributions, these should be disbursed according to the directives in the Final Order.

Completion of the Probate Process

The successful completion of Stage 6 not only involves the physical distribution of the estate's assets but also the meticulous documentation and filing required to legally conclude the probate process. The personal representative's thorough and transparent handling of this stage ensures that the estate is closed efficiently and that they are fully released from their duties without any lingering liabilities. This final discharge by the court marks the official end of the probate case.

Stage 6: Distribution and Discharge ™

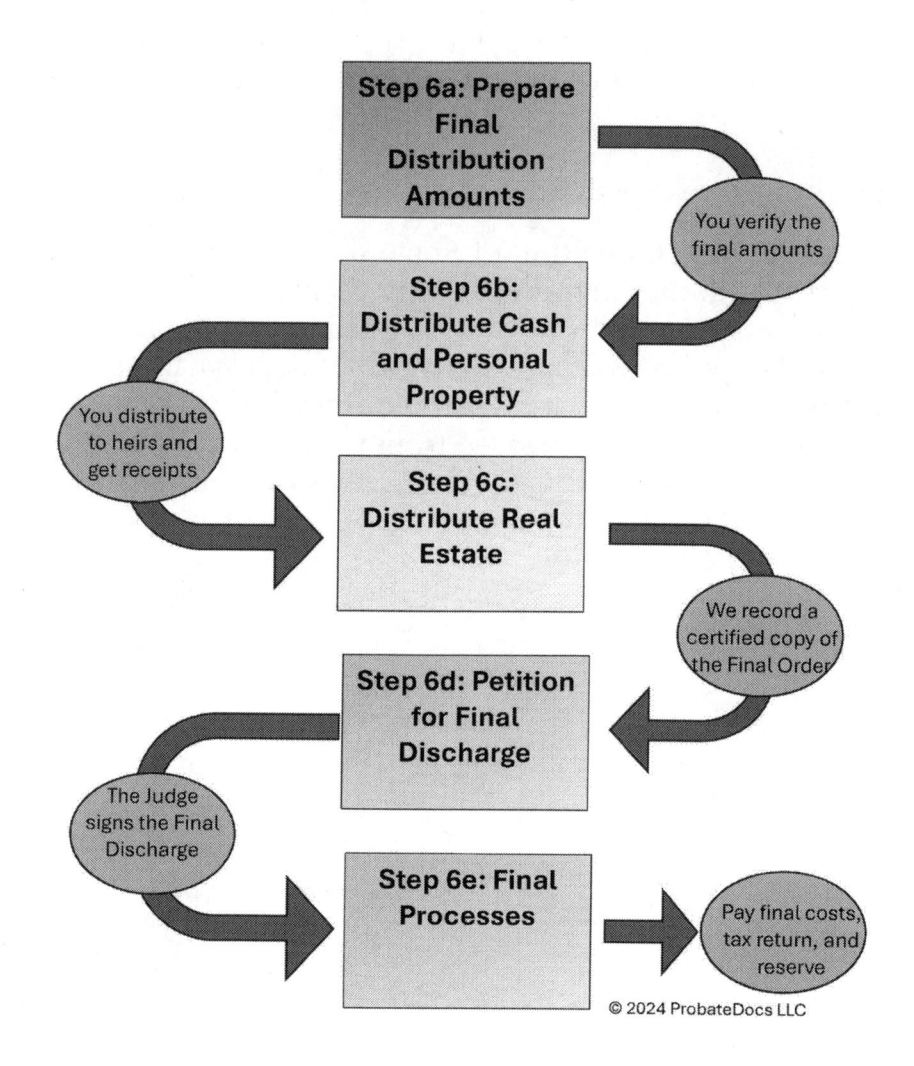

Step 6a: Prepare Final Distribution Amounts

You verify the final amounts

Step 6b: Distribute Cash and Personal Property

You distribute to heirs and get receipts

Step 6c: Distribute Real Estate

We record a certified copy of the Final Order

Step 6d: Petition for Final Discharge

The Judge signs the Final Discharge

Step 6e: Final Processes

Pay final costs, tax return, and reserve

© 2024 ProbateDocs LLC

Stage 6: Distribution and Discharge ™

Step	Tasks to Complete	What WE do	What YOU do	Estimated Time Frame
6a	Prepare Final Distribute Amounts	We draft a Final Distribution for You to sign	You verify the exact bank balance and review and sign the Final Distribution	Time varies, with complexity of Your case and when You gather information and documents
6b	Distribute Cash and Personal Property	We draft receipts based on the Final Distribution and Form W-9 for You to give to each heir	You write checks, distribute the funds and personal property, and You gather signed receipts and Form W-9	Time varies, with when You distribute and get the receipts and Form W-9
6c	Distribute Real Estate	We get a certified copy of the Order for Distribution, We record it with the County Recorder (We pay recording fees from Your deposit)	You gather signed receipts and Form W-9	Within five business days of having the certified Order for Distribution
6d	Petition for Final Discharge	We draft an Ex Parte Petition for Final Discharge and file it with the receipts with the Court (We pay the eFiling fee from Your deposit)	You give Us the receipts and You sign the Ex Parte Petition for Final Discharge	Processing times may vary as the Court may take some time to process
6e	Final Processes	We get the Final Discharge signed by the judge and send to the Bond Company to exonerate the bond, We close Our file	You file a final estate income tax return, pay final bills, contact the tax assessor regarding supplemental property tax bills, pay the annual bond premium, and distribute the reserve, close estate bank account	Time varies as the Judge may take some time to process the Final Discharge, complexity of Your case and when You complete the final processes

© 2024 ProbateDocs LLC

Distribution and Final Discharge

When wrapping up a probate case, finalizing the distribution of the estate's assets is a detailed process. Here's a comprehensive explanation of the steps involved, incorporating the information you've provided:

145

Final Petition Approval and Order for Distribution

Once the court approves the final petition and signs the order for distribution, it authorizes the personal representative to distribute the estate's assets according to the will or state laws.

Verification of Amounts

Before disbursing funds:

1. Verify Bills and Inheritance Amounts: The personal representative needs to verify how much each heir will receive and ensure all estate bills are accounted for. This includes confirming the total amount available after settling debts and any specific bequests mentioned in the will.

Preparing for Distribution

2. Preparation of Receipts: Prepare receipts for heirs to sign upon receiving their inheritance. This documentation is crucial to prove that heirs have received their designated assets.
3. Tax Documentation: Distribute IRS Form W-9 to heirs to collect appropriate information for tax reporting purposes. This form is necessary for the estate to report any potentially taxable transactions related to the distribution.

Sending Distributions

4. Send Checks and Tax Forms: Mail the checks and IRS Form W-9 to heirs. Instruct heirs to return the signed Form W-9 to ensure proper tax documentation is filed.

Court Filing and Final Steps

5. File Receipts and Final Discharge Petition: Once all distributions are made, and signed receipts are collected, file

these receipts with the court. Also, submit an Ex Parte Petition for Final Discharge to the court, requesting the release of the personal representative from their duties.
6. Probate Bond Exoneration: Send a copy of the Ex Parte Petition for Final Discharge to the bond company to initiate the exoneration of the probate bond.

Managing Reserve Funds

7. Maintain a Reserve: Keep a reserve of funds from the estate to cover final expenses such as:

- Overnight mail costs for sending checks to heirs.
- Potential supplemental property tax bills.
- Costs associated with preparing the estate's final income tax return.
- Probate bond premiums.
- Fees for recording real estate transfers, if applicable.

8. Handling Property Taxes and Other Costs: Before using reserve funds, ensure all necessary payments are made. Check with the county tax assessor about potential reassessment of property and associated taxes.

Threshold for Court Accounting

9. Accounting for the Reserve: If the amount held in reserve exceeds a certain threshold (which varies by county), you will need to account to the court for how these funds were used, along with providing receipts. If it is below the threshold, detailed court accounting might not be required, but maintaining records is still advised.

By following these detailed steps, the personal representative ensures that all aspects of the estate closure are handled legally and transparently, leading to the proper distribution of the inheritance and the successful conclusion of the probate process.

GLOSSARY OF COMMON PROBATE TERMS IN SIMPLE LANGUAGE

A

Administrator: A person appointed by the court to manage and distribute the estate of someone who died without a will.

Affidavit: A written statement confirmed by oath or affirmation, used as evidence in court.

Age of Majority: The age when someone gains the rights and responsibilities of being an adult, which in California is 18 years or older.

Amended: To add to or change a document that has been filed in court by replacing it in its entirety with a new version. In Probate, an Amended Petition will be given a new hearing date.

Ancillary Administration. Administration in a state other than the decedent's domicile, when there is also a known administration at the place of domicile.

Assets: Everything owned by a person at the time of their death, including money, property, and personal belongings.

Attestation Clause. The clause generally at the end of a will wherein the witnesses certify that the will has been signed by the testator before them, and the manner of its signing. A certificate certifying as to the facts and circumstances of the signing of a will.

B

Beneficiary: A person or organization entitled to receive a share of the estate, as named in the will or determined by law.

Bequeath: The legal term used to leave someone personal property in a will,

Bequest: The legal term used to describe personal property left in a will.

Blocked Account: A bank account for the decedent's estate that is court ordered to be blocked in which withdrawals can only be made with a court order for withdrawal.

Bond: A form of insurance that the executor or administrator may be required to obtain to protect the estate from mismanagement. The annual premium for the bond that must be paid each year.

Bond Rider. A document that is an addendum to a bond changes the terms of the original bond's terms, such as increasing the amount of the bond or changing the title of the personal representative from Special Administrator to Administrator.

C

Certified Copy: An official copy of a court document that is notated as a true, complete, and authentic representation of the original document.

Citation: A court-issued writ that commands a person to appear at a certain time and place to do something demanded in the writ, or to show cause for not doing so. An order or summons notifying a proposed conservatee of the petition being made, and or commanding the person to appear in court.

Codicil: A legal document that makes changes or additions to an existing will.

Commissioner: A bench officer appointed by the court who is given the power to hear and make decisions concerning certain limited legal matters.

Community Property: Generally, property acquired by a couple during their marriage except by gift or inheritance.

Conflict of Interest: Refers to a situation when someone, such as a lawyer or public official, has competing professional or personal obligations or personal or financial interests that would make it difficult to fulfill his/her duties fairly.

Contested: To defend against an adverse claim made in a court by a petitioner; to challenge a petition or the admission of a will to probate.

Creditor: A person or organization that is owed money by the deceased as of the date of death. Except that the person that paid the funeral expenses is also a creditor, even if they paid the funeral costs after death.

Creditor's Claim: A document wherein a creditor demands payment for debt owed by the decedent.

D

Decedent: The person who has died.

Declaration: A written statement that is unsworn but made under penalty of perjury. All declarations must be dated, state the place of execution, and signed under penalty of perjury under the laws of the state of California.

Debt: Money owed by the decedent to creditors.

Deed. A written legal document that describes a piece of property and outlines its boundaries. The seller of a property transfers ownership by delivering the deed to the buyer in exchange for an agreed upon sum of money.

Devise: A legal term that now means any real or personal property that is transferred under the terms of a will. Previously, the term only referred to real property.

Devisee: A person or entity who receives real or personal property under the terms of a will.

Disbursements: The act of paying out money, commonly from a fund or in settlement of a debt or account payable.

Discharge: The term used to describe the court order releasing the personal representative from any further duties regarding the estate being subjected to probate proceedings, and the form to use is an Ex Parte Petition for Final Discharge and Order. This typically occurs when the duties have been completed but can also happen in the middle of the probate proceeding when the executor or administrator wishes to withdraw or is removed.

Distributee: Someone who receives property from an estate.

Domicile: Generally, domicile is where a person lives, and where they intend to be their home.

E

Encumbrances: Any mortgage, deed of trust, or lien against real estate.

Equity: The difference between the fair market value of your real and personal property and the amount you still owe on it, if any.

Escheat: A legal doctrine under which property belonging to a deceased person with no heirs passes to the state.

Estate: All the money, property, and personal belongings owned by the decedent at the time of death.

Executor: A person named in the will to manage and distribute the estate.

Expenses of Administration: The costs incurred by a personal representative in carrying out the terms of a will or in administering an estate. These include probate court fees, eFiling fees, house utilities, mortgage payments, taxes, fees charged by an executor or administrator, attorney's fees, and appraiser's fees.

F

Fair Market Value: That price for which an item of property would be purchased by a willing buyer, and sold by a willing seller, both knowing all the facts and neither being under any compulsion to buy or sell.

Fiduciary: A person who has the responsibility to manage someone else's money or property with care and loyalty.

Fiduciary Duty: An obligation to act in the best interest of another party. For instance, a corporation's board member has a fiduciary duty to the shareholders, a trustee has a fiduciary duty to the trust's beneficiaries, and an attorney has a fiduciary duty to a client.

Formal Probate: A court-supervised process of administering the estate, including proving the will, paying debts, and distributing assets.

Full Authority Under the Independent Administration of Estate Act: The Probate Code allows for a personal representative to act with limited authority or full authority under the Independent Administration of Estate Acts (IAEA). A personal representative with full authority under the IAEA can perform many acts without seeking court approval but may have to give a Notice of Proposed Action to give a 15-day opportunity for any heir or beneficiary to object to the proposed action. A personal representative with limited authority under the IAEA must seek court approval for most actions.

Funeral Expenses: The costs of burial, headstone, cremation, funeral, memorial, etc. To seek reimbursement for Funeral Expenses from the estate, you must file a creditor claim within the specified time limits.

G

General Personal Representative: Someone appointed to generally administer the entire estate. This does not include a Special Administrator.

Grantor: The person who creates a trust.

Guardian: A person legally appointed to manage the personal and/or financial affairs of a minor or incapacitated person.

H

Heir (Heir at Law): A person legally entitled to inherit property from the decedent if there is no will.

Holographic Will: A will that is handwritten and signed by the person making it, without witnesses.

I

Independent Administration of Estate Act: The Probate Code allows for a personal representative to act with limited authority or full authority under the Independent Administration of Estate Acts (IAEA). A personal representative with full authority under the IAEA can perform many acts without seeking court approval but may have to give a Notice of Proposed Action to give a 15-day opportunity for any heir or beneficiary to object to the proposed action. A personal representative with limited authority under the IAEA must seek court approval for most actions.

Intestate: Dying without a legal will.

Inventory and Appraisal: A detailed list of all assets and debts of the estate for appraisal by the Probate Referee.

Issue: The lineal descendants (biological children, adopted children, grandchildren, great-grandchildren etc.) of a person.

J

Judicial Council Forms: The Judicial Council of California has created many forms (called "Judicial Council forms") to standardize the preparation of court documents. The Judicial Council forms that are labeled "mandatory" must be used and the forms that are labeled "optional" are only optional to use.

L

Letters: A legal document issued by the court authorizing a personal representative to manage and distribute the estate. Since there are four different types of Letters that the court can issue, the word "Letters" is a generic form of any of the Letters issued by the court.

Letters of Administration: A legal document issued by the court in an intestate estate authorizing the administrator to manage and distribute the estate.

Letters of Administration with Will Annexed: A legal document issued by the court authorizing a person, who is not nominated as the executor, to manage and distribute the estate.

Letters of Special Administration: A legal document issued by the court temporarily authorizing the personal representative to manage the estate in an emergency basis. A special administrator only has certain powers given by the Probate Code and the specific powers given by the judge.

Letters Testamentary: A legal document issued by the court authorizing the appointed executor to manage and distribute the estate.

Limited Authority Under the Independent Administration of Estate Act: The Probate Code allows for a personal representative to act with limited authority or full authority under the Independent Administration of Estate Acts (IAEA). A personal representative with full authority under the IAEA can perform many acts without seeking court approval, but may have to give a Notice of Proposed Action to give a 15-day opportunity for any heir or beneficiary to object to the proposed action. A personal representative with limited authority under the IAEA must seek court approval for most actions.

Lost Will: When the original will cannot be found, it is a Lost Will. The Probate Code presumes that a Lost Will was destroyed with the intent to revoke it if it was last in the possession of the testator and the testator had capacity. The presumption can be overcome with sufficient explanation.

M

Minor: A person that is under the age of 18 years old. The term does not apply to an emancipated youth.

N

Next of Kin: The closest living relatives of the decedent.

Notice: Information given to a person or entity of some act done, or about to be done, including the date, time, and place of a court hearing, if any.

Notice of Proposed Action: A document mailed out by the personal representative giving the heirs, beneficiaries, or anyone else entitled to Notice, that the personal representative intends to perform an action unless anyone objects within fifteen days. The most common type of Notice of Proposed Action is the sale of real estate by a personal representative with full authority under the IAEA.

O

Order to Show Cause (OSC): Court order commanding a person to appear in court at a specific date and time, and to give a reason to the court's satisfaction why he or she should not be compelled to perform a certain act (or cease a certain act). A declaration to the court is filed before the court hearing on the order to show cause.

P

Petition: A formal request to the court for a specific action, such as starting probate proceedings.

Personal Property: Items of tangible or intangible property that are not real estate or attached to the land.

Personal Representative: Another term for the executor or administrator responsible for managing the estate.

Petition: A written, formal request, properly filed with the court, for a specific action or order, such as a Petition for Probate to appoint a personal representative of the decedent's estate.

Petitioner: One who presents a petition to a court. The person who opposes the prayer of the petition is called the "respondent" or "objector."

Pour Over Will: A will that gives some or all assets of the decedent to a trust.

Probate: The legal process of administering the estate of a deceased person, including proving the will, paying debts, and distributing assets.

Probate Estate: All the assets owned at death that require some form of legal proceeding before title may be transferred to the proper heirs. Property that passes automatically at death (property in trust, life insurance proceeds, property in a "pay-on-death" account or property held in joint tenancy) is not in the probate estate.

Probate Examiner: The Probate Examiner works at the court and examines files and documents in pending probate matters set for hearing, providing technical, procedural and legal review to ensure that matters before the court have proper notice and complete documents for a court ruling. The Examiner's work-product is then posted prior to the hearing date in Probate Notes for the parties to review and correct deficiencies (or defects) prior to the hearing.

Probate Notes: This can be questions, deficiencies, that are noted by the Probate Examiner to a Petition that have to be cleared up before the court will approve the Petition.

Probate Referee: The appraiser who is appointed by the court to appraise the assets of the decedent's estate with an Inventory and Appraisal.

Proof of Service: The form filed with the court that proves the date on which documents were formally served on a party in a court action.

Public Administrator: The county department that will administer an estate if there is no one else to administer the estate.

Publication: A newspaper publication is required to give sufficient notice to any potential creditors of the decedent.

R

Real Property: Real estate or anything attached to the land, such as a building or house.

Receipts In Accounting: All cash or other assets of the estate received by the personal representative, other than those listed on the inventory and appraisement. Receipts must be reported to the court on a schedule in the periodic accounting.

Receipts For Distribution: The document signed by the distributee showing proof that the funds were distributed by the personal representative.

Residue: The remaining assets of the estate after all debts, taxes, and specific bequests have been paid.

Respondent: The person against who opposes a petition.

Revocable Trust: A trust that can be changed or revoked by the grantor during their lifetime.

S

Self-Proving Will: A will is self-proving when it has certain language signed under penalty of perjury by the witnesses.

Statute: Any written law passed by a state or federal legislative body.

Stipulation: An agreement between parties or their attorneys.

Successor Trustee: A person or institution named to manage a trust after the original trustee dies or becomes unable to act.

Summary Probate: A simplified probate process for small estates that meet certain criteria.

Supplement: Something added to complete a thing, make up for a deficiency, or extend or strengthen the whole. In Probate, these are generally filed to correct defects noted by the Probate Examiner.

Surcharge: A money judgment which the court can impose on the fiduciary if the fiduciary's improper acts cause a loss to the estate.

T

Testate: When someone dies leaving a legal will.

Testator: A person who has made a valid will.

Title: Ownership of property.

Trust: A legal arrangement where one person (trustee) holds and manages property for the benefit of another (beneficiary).

Trustee: The person named in a trust document who will manage the property owned by the trust and distributes any income according to the document. A trustee can be an individual or a corporate fiduciary.

U

Uniform Transfer to Minors Act: California law, which provides a way for someone to give or leave property to a minor by appointing a "custodian" to manage the property for the minor.

V

Vesting: Expression of the form of legal title by which property is held, usually in a deed. An example of a vesting is "husband and wife, as joint tenants."

W

Will: A legal document that states how a person's property should be distributed after their death.

Will Contest: A proceeding peculiar to probate for the determination of questions of construction of a will or whether there is or is not a will. Any kind of litigated controversy concerning the eligibility of an instrument to probate as distinguished from validity of the contents of the will. (Will contests are in rem proceedings in that the contest is brought against the thing, the will, as opposed to in personam proceedings, which are brought against a person.)

Witness: A person who observes the signing of a will and attests to its authenticity.

Made in the USA
Columbia, SC
04 December 2024